DEVOTIONS
FOR
DIETERS

Also by Charlie Shedd

To help you manage your life . . .
The Fat Is in Your Head
Time for All Things: Ten Affirmations for Christian Use of Time

For young people . . .
The Stork Is Dead
You Are Somebody Special (edited by Charlie Shedd)
How to Know If You're Really in Love

On marriage . . .
Letters to Karen: On Keeping Love in Marriage
Letters to Philip: On How to Treat a Woman
Talk to Me
The Best Dad Is a Good Lover
Celebration in the Bedroom (coauthored with Martha Shedd)
How to Stay in Love (coauthored with Martha Shedd)

For parents and grandparents. . .
You Can Be a Great Parent
Smart Dads I Know
A Dad Is for Spending Time With
Grandparents: Then God Created Grandparents and It Was Very
   Good
Grandparents' Family Book

Ideas for churches
The Exciting Church: Where People Really Pray
The Exciting Church: Where They Give Their Money Away
The Exciting Church: Where They Really Use the Bible

Cassette Resource Kits . . .
Fun Family Forum
Straight Talk on Love, Sex, and Marriage
Good times with the Bible

DEVOTIONS FOR DIETERS

Charlie W. Shedd

WORD BOOKS
PUBLISHER
WACO, TEXAS

A DIVISION OF
WORD, INCORPORATED

Library of Congress Cataloging in Publication Data:

Shedd, Charlie W.

Devotions for dieters.
1. Dieters—Prayer-books and devotions—English. I. Title.
BV4596.D53S48 1983   242'.86   83–10272
ISBN 0–8499–0330–0

Printed in the United States of America

Scripture quotations marked as indicated are from the following versions: ASV: The American Standard Version of the Bible, 1901, published by Thomas Nelson & Sons. Berkeley: The Modern Language Bible: The New Berkeley Version in Modern English, copyright © 1945, 1959, 1969 by Zondervan Publishing House. Goodspeed: The Bible: An American Translation by Edgar J. Goodspeed, J. Powis Smith, et al., copyright © 1923, 1935, 1948 by the University of Chicago. JB: The Jerusalem Bible, copyright © 1966 by Darton, Longman & Todd Ltd. and Doubleday & Company, Inc. JWNT: John Wesley's New Testament, 1953, published by John C. Winston Co., Philadelphia. Knox: The Holy Bible, translated by Ronald Knox, copyright 1944, 1948, 1950 by Sheed and Ward, Inc., New York. KJV: The King James Version of the Bible. Lamsa: The Holy Bible from Ancient Eastern Manuscripts by George M. Lamsa, copyright © 1940, 1957, 1961 by A. J. Holman Company, a subsidiary of J. B. Lippincott Company. Moffatt: A New Translation of the Bible by James Moffatt, copyright © 1954 by James Moffatt. NAS: The New American Standard Bible, copyright © 1960, 1962, 1963 by The Lockman Foundation. NEB: The New English Bible, copyright The Delegates of the Oxford University Press and The Syndics of the Cambridge University Press, 1961, 1970. Norlie: The New Testament: A New Translation by Olaf M. Norlie, copyright © 1961 by Zondervan Publishing House. NTBE: The New Testament in Basic English, published by Cambridge University Press in association with Evans Bros. Ltd. Phillips: The New Testament in Modern English by J. B. Phillips, published by The MacMillan Company, © 1958, 1960, 1972 by J. B. Phillips. Rieu: The Four Gospels translated by E. V. Rieu, copyright © 1953 by Penguin Press, Ltd. RSV: The Revised Standard Version of the Bible, copyright © 1946, 1952, © 1971 and 1973 by the Division of Christian Education of the National Council of the Churches of Christ in the U.S.A. TCNT: The Twentieth Century New Testament, published by Moody Bible Institute. TEV: Today's English Version of the Bible, copyright © American Bible Society 1966, 1971, 1976. TLB: The Living Bible, Paraphrased, published by Tyndale House Publishers, 1971, Wheaton, Ill. Weymouth: The New Testament in Modern Speech by Richard Francis Weymouth, published by the Pilgrim Press, 1943. Williams: The New Testament in the Language of the People by Charles B. Williams, copyright 1949 by Moody Press.

To Martha
   who, though a non-fatty,
   has been my fellow struggler
      for forty years.
      Thank you, svelte friend,
      I think we're going to win.

Contents

Abbreviations used in this book

ASV	The American Standard Version of the Bible
Berkeley	*The Modern Language Bible: The New Berkeley Version in Modern English*
Goodspeed	*The Bible: An American Translation* by Edgar J. Goodspeed
JB	*The Jerusalem Bible*
JWNT	*John Wesley's New Testament*
Knox	*The Holy Bible: A Translation from the Latin Vulgate in the Light of the Hebrew and Greek Originals* by Ronald Knox
KJV	The King James Version of the Bible
Lamsa	*The Holy Bible from Ancient Eastern Manuscripts* by George M. Lamsa
Moffatt	*A New Translation of the Bible* by James Moffatt
NAS	*The New American Standard Bible*
NEB	*The New English Bible*
Norlie	*The New Testament: A New Translation* by Olaf M. Norlie
NTBE	*The New Testament in Basic English*
Phillips	*The New Testament in Modern English* by J. B. Phillips
Rieu	*The Four Gospels* by E. V. Rieu
RSV	The Revised Standard Version of the Bible
TCNT	*The Twentieth Century New Testament*
TLB	*The Living Bible, Paraphrased*
Weymouth	*The New Testament in Modern Speech* by Richard Francis Weymouth
Williams	*The New Testament in the Language of the People* by Charles B. Williams

Preface

This book is about you and losing weight and the Bible. *Devotions for Dieters* is for Christians. Or shouldn't we say it is for those of us trying to be Christian? Every honest heavy knows what that means. We've tried and tried and tried. Most of us have tried most everything.

Diets, drugs, pills, shots.

Workshops, seminars, institutes, clubs.

Equipment, springs, levers, pads, belts, weights.

Fasting, semi-fasting, total fasting.

Hypnotism, acupuncture.

Advice, promotions, movements, spas.

Even full page ads we've tried.

Fine print, tight copy, words,

words, words, and here at the end:

"Send $9.99. We'll give you the answer."

Will they? Will all the techniques of

Madison Avenue, harnessed to take us in,

give us the answer?

Answer: No. For the likes of us the final answer is the Lord's answer, and out of his Book he speaks. To us he speaks with weighted words for our weighty needs. Then, when his Book is silent, he speaks by the Living Word. That's what he said he'd do, and he does. "I am the truth," he said, and by his Holy Spirit he promises that if we listen he will bring us to the truth. General truth, specific truth, personal truth, all truth.

11

Throughout this book, Scripture references will be from many translations and numerous versions. Some marked "C&M" have a special meaning. For thirty years at our house we have been studying God's Word together, searching the Scripture as husband and wife. Be it known right now that we are not Bible scholars, but Bible students we are. And one of the greatest joys which can come to any two students of Scripture together is confidence at last to write their own interpretation. That is the background of the "C&M." Meaning: Charlie and Martha hear it like this.

Meditations, reflections, thoughts, musings, texts, passages, characters, stories from God's Word can help us remain somewhere in the range of proper proportions.

In the yackety yak of all the voices around us—selling, advising, cajoling—we do need a final word.

That's what God's Word has become for this one fatty—the final Word.

May *Devotions for Dieters* help you to see that his Word can be your final word too.

CHARLIE SHEDD
Fripp Island,
South Carolina

12

THE ORIGINAL ME

"Isn't it amazing how God put me together? Sometimes I feel it in my heart."

Psalm 139:13—14, C&M

What was I like in the beginning?

My big bones. Or are they?

Perfect?

What was I like in the beginning?

"Isn't it amazing how God put me together?
Sometimes I feel it in my heart."
Psalm 139:13–14, C&M

"You made all the delicate, inner parts of my body,
and knit them together in my mother's womb. . . . It
is amazing to think about. Your workmanship is
marvelous—and how well I know it."
verses 13–14, TLB

"It was you who created my inmost self, and put me
together in my mother's womb; for all these mysteries
I thank you; for the wonder of myself."
verses 13–14, JB

"We are fearfully and wonderfully made."
verse 14, KJV

WHAT DID I LOOK LIKE when the Lord first dreamed of me?

Our friend Homer is one of the most dynamic witnesses we know. He's a big man with a big grin. Lights come on inside as he talks, and everything about him seems to glow. Even his bald head seems to glow. And especially he glows as he describes how he whipped his drinking problem to reach his years of sobriety.

I have always had a special appreciation for alcoholics who

have learned to control their intake by total abstinence. True, those of us who are foodaholics have a somewhat different problem. We can't quit eating altogether, or at least not permanently. Yet when we are thinking straight, we understand. Over-consumers of every kind can readily identify with and be grateful for all fellow strugglers who share this road.

How did Homer do it?

I like his answer, and you will too.

He said, "You really should be asking, 'How *am* I doing it?' And of course, there's no simple answer, but let's start here. I have this special little prayer I pray late in the evening. When my family has gone to bed and I'm sitting alone in my big chair, I get very quiet. Then I pray, 'Lord, show me Homer the way you first dreamed of Homer. I want to see me the way you thought of me in the original.'

"Would you believe sometimes I do get the picture? Not often, but often enough, and when it comes, it's absolutely beautiful. That's what I want to be—beautiful like the Lord first dreamed of me."*

Always there have been doomsayers tracing mankind back to the fall of Adam, womankind to the sin of Eve: "Behold the negatives. Isn't it awful?"

Now any realistic son of Adam, any honest daughter of Eve will say, "I too am among the negatives, and it is awful. Awful I have been, awful I am, awful I fear I'm going to be. But is this the real me?"

---

* Homer's simple prayer has been one of the most profound influences in this one fatty's pilgrimage to proper contours. Because it means so much to me, I have used it before in previous writings, the most recent of which is *Grandparent's Family Book: A Keepsake for Our Grandchild*, (New York: Doubleday & Co., 1983).

16

To which comes the Good News. No! This is not the real me. Genesis 1 tells us exactly how we were in the beginning:

> So God created man in his own image, in the image of God created he him; male and female created he them. . . . And God saw everything he had made, and behold, it was very good (vv. 27, 31, KJV).

In the beginning then, man, woman, boy, girl, grandpa, grandma, aunts, uncles, cousins, the whole human race, me—all of us were wrought by the hand of a wonderful Creator and stamped with his image.

When I start with the Bible where the Bible starts, I start where I must start—back with the original me.

> *Prayer:*
> *Lord, show me what I was when you first dreamed of me. Size? Shape? Your hopes for me? That's what I want to be.*
>
> *Amen*

17

Amazing thought:

In the interior of me
God has engraved his likeness.

My big bones. Or are they?

"He knoweth our frame."
Psalm 103:14, KJV

CHARTS. THESE WE HAVE ALWAYS with us. Charts on the fat man's chances. Charts on the fat lady's too. Chances for heart attack, chances for diabetes, chances for back problems, kidney problems, eye problems, dental problems. Calorie charts, vitamin charts, mineral charts, charts on body chemistry. Interesting charts, scary charts, all kinds of charts—and especially charts on frame, bones, body structure. Somewhere there are charts on all of these—and they all have to do with how much we weigh, and what we *should* weigh.

I saw one again this week. In the hospital waiting room, a giant chart. Begin over here at the height column. Six foot male, big frame. Ideal weight? Range him from here to here. Female, five-three—this much for the lady. See? Pick your height, figure your frame, run your eye over chart; now you know. This much you should weigh.

Says who?

Says the insurance company, mostly. (Don't you sometimes wonder if insurance companies pick only the ultra skinny to head their chart departments?)

So where do we go from here? Where I went this summer was down with a dull thud. I was visiting my friend David in California. He's an M.D. who practices holistic medicine and he's written a very fine book about it.*I like the holistic approach, so once each year when we're out his way, Martha and I check in with David. His examination is thorough, kind, honest, probing. Listen, analyze, examine, check and check again. Microscope, stethoscope, then bring in the charts. Now tell it like it is. And this is the way it is, "Charlie, you've been operating on the delusion that you are big frame. You're not. Not big. Not extra big. Medium! See? This is a medical tape measure. Here it is, right here on the chart. Medium!"

And like the man says, all these years I have been living with the delusion, "Big frame me! Maybe even extra big." Does it matter? Any fatty who has weighed too much too long knows how much it matters. Ten pounds, twenty pounds, thirty pounds—that's how much it matters. It means this many more pounds down to the ideal weight.

Dull, dull thud!

---

* David Messenger, *Dr. Messenger's Guide to Better Health* (Old Tappan, N.J.: Fleming H. Revell, 1981).

Certain scholars of the Psalms change the word in Psalm 103:14 from *frame* to *bones:* "He knoweth our bones." Yet even a linguistic picky could come by little comfort from that change. In the original, *frame* and *bones* are the same word.

So any way we read it, today's verse leads us again to the facing of facts, and this is today's hard fact: Our Creator knows!

Certain Psalms might well be called the *"all* that is within me" Psalms. Psalm 103 opens with "Bless the Lord, O my soul, and *all* that is within me" (kjv). *All!* No exceptions, every part. Soul, mind, body, muscles, nerves, tendons, bones—every single part of us exists for this one reason: to bless the Lord!

And how can we possibly bless the Lord on a false assumption? We can't. What can we do? We can begin this day re-tracking our minds to bless the Lord. From big-bone thinking to medium thinking to small thinking we must ask for *his* thinking. "He knoweth our frame."

> *Prayer:*
>
> *Heavenly Father, you know it all. You know how many pounds you planned for me. You know my bones and what they were meant to carry. Show me today what I was, what I am, what I should be. I want to look right in your sight.*
>
> *This is my prayer: "Bless the Lord, all his works in all places of his dominion" (Ps. 103:22, kjv)—including me.*
>
> *Amen*

Questionnaire on my frame

1. In my thinking up to now I have considered my frame size:

   Extra large _____
   Large _____
   Medium _____
   Small _____
   Petite _____

2. I have _____, have not _____ had a doctor tell me what he thinks.

3. Meditating on Psalm 103, I do want to know exactly what God wants me to be. Yes _____ No _____

4. I will seek out someone who can show me by actual measurements whether I have been thinking right about my frame. In the very near future I will get an accurate reading and set a goal based on that report. Yes _____ No _____ Maybe _____

Note: The writer of Psalm 103 promises two specific rewards for shaping up (v. 5):

First: *satisfaction of appetite*—"[He] satisfieth thy mouth with good things . . ." (KJV).

Second: *renewed youth*—". . . thy youth is renewed like the eagle's" (KJV).

Perfect?

"Be ye therefore perfect."
Matthew 5:48, KJV

PERFECT? ME? Oh come now, "perfect" is only for Jesus. Yet here he is today assigning that role to me: "<u>Be ye therefore perfect</u>."

It is so tempting to pigeonhole this all-inclusive verse. Anyone knows perfection is impossible. Put it aside, put it out of reach. Actually, if we do choose to pigeonhole this verse, certain scholars seem to back us up. "This is only a goal," they say, "Jesus knows we will never be perfect. But go for it anyway, stretch, try like crazy."

So what is the real message? The message, I think, is, *"Charlie, you be the perfect you."* Which comes out exactly where we began. "Be the self which God intended. That's the perfect you!"

For all of us girthy followers this verse has extensive ramifications. Most fellow strugglers I know come from backgrounds heavy with perfectionism. Father, mother, teacher, preacher— someone—laid it on us: "Do it right, you hear? And I do mean right."

Karen Horney, the German psychiatrist, in her book *Our Inner Conflicts,* * gives us an interesting picture of childhood. In every one of us, she says, there is a worthwhile self struggling to reach its potential. She calls this goal self-actualization, and with no exception every one of us, in her opinion, is born with the drive to achieve it (shades of Gen. 1, Ps. 139:14).

If we can accept Dr. Horney's premise or begin where Genesis 1 begins, we can readily see where we are headed: conflict! We want to be ourselves, yes. Yet we also want to keep "them" happy—"them" as in mother, as in father, as in teacher, as in the whole wide world. So we strain, struggle, give it fits, "Be ye therefore perfect."

Then as we grew older, we began to see the impossibility here. So let us try another approach, we will become aggressive. If we can get control, there will be no conflict. We will be in charge. Let us now become a holy terror, scare them silly, wear them to a frazzle. Most of us have memories of going through that stage.

But since aggressiveness is not as satisfactory as it promised, some of us opt for another way. Why not detach ourselves,

---

* (New York: W. W. Norton, 1945), Part I, pp. 48–73.

build walls, keep our distance? If "they" have no access to our real thoughts, there will be no conflict.

On and on our efforts go—sometimes one way, sometimes another, sometimes a combination. Be compliant, be aggressive, be detached. Be some of each or be them all. But always padding along beside us comes this other little fellow crying, "Oh, to be me."

No wonder some of us had such a hard time growing up! Or shouldn't we say, "No wonder we're *having* such a hard time"? And small wonder other people are too. Weird behavior, psychosis, depression, mania, drugs, alcohol, ruptured relationships; aren't they all in part an attempt to escape the false selves hounding us? Hounding us from our history, hounding us right now, hounding us from where we seem to be going. Could it be that overeating is one of life's attempts to satisfy the false selves, to quiet the false urges?

It is a great verse for fatties: "Be ye therefore perfect," a massive theme with massive significance. This I must study, maybe for forty years, until I begin to see what I was meant to be in God's sight.

> *Prayer:*
> *Lord Jesus, you are the great emancipator. Somewhere in the murky crevices of me there are many attempts to be somebody else's idea of perfect. I want you to live in me. Set me free. Free from the phonies—the phony influences, the phony selves, the phony struggle.*
> *This day I would be the perfect me for the perfect you.*
>
> *Amen*

25

THE LORD'S PRAYER

Amazing how familiar passages speak specifically to specific needs.

How many times have I prayed the Lord's Prayer? And how many times have I really meant it?

No way to count those answers, but this I know: Whenever I pray the Lord's Prayer and mean it, out of the old familiar he brings new truths. (Note: The Lord's Prayer is to be found in Matthew 6 and Luke 11.)

Am I looking for heaven where it isn't?

I must quit being nervous about tomorrow's bread.

All my grudges make me hungry.

So many temptations everywhere

Am I looking for heaven where it isn't?

> *"Our Father which art in heaven."*
> *Matthew 6:9,* KJV

THE HEAVENLY SMORGASBORD! Miles and miles of food. And me? I'm at the dessert counter, spending my first thousand years of eternity eating creamy desserts.

Ludicrous? Of course. But when I even breathe such foolish fantasy with any group of fellow strugglers, would you believe? Everyone is right there with me. Under our avoirdupois, and not far under either, is the heavenly dream in which we eat and eat. We eat and eat and eat and never mind the pounds, never gain an ounce. Or if we do, who cares? This is heaven.

29

One of our favorite fantasies on the marquee of forever and ever is: "Groceries Galore In Glory!"

Harmless sort of entertainment? Maybe. Maybe not. One of my funny preacher friends is fond of saying, "It's hell if you don't make heaven." Strange turn of thought, but Jesus said something like that.

Any student of the Christly teachings knows how much emphasis he placed on the hereafter. He also warned that we could miss the eternal kingdom. And because that's true, he said we are wise to be living now so that we will inherit it. But interwoven with all these teachings is his assurance too that heaven can begin right now. How? By living right now in accord with his lordship.

For us fatties that means at least one thing we do not like. We do not like the fact that our route to heaven now is straight past those creamy desserts to the salad counter. Straight to the health foods. Straight to eating each meal and every bite with him.

There are only two words repeated in the Lord's Prayer. One of these is *kingdom:* "Thy kingdom come" and "Thine is the kingdom." Double reference number two is *heaven:* "Our Father which art in heaven" and "Thy will be done in earth, as it is in heaven" (all KJV).

Rule for Bible students: *Whenever Jesus doubles up his words in one short teaching, these words are worth our double attention.*

Why does he say them twice? Why does he put them together?

One answer has to be that when "the kingdoms of this world are become the kingdoms of our Lord and of his Christ"

(Rev. 11:15, KJV), that will be heaven. Earnestly then we pray and mean it, "Thy kingdom come. Thy will be done in earth, as it is in heaven." But do we also mean, "Thy kingdom come. Thy will be done in *me?*"

> *Lord, when I pray, "Our Father which art in heaven, Hallowed be thy name," I really do mean what I pray. I want all people everywhere to reverence you, to love you. With all my heart I mean what I pray.*
>> *Yes* _____
>> *No* _____
>> *Including me* _____
>> *With certain reservations* _____

> *Lord, when I pray, "Thy kingdom come. Thy will be done," I mean that too. Starting right here, at the center of my soul, I yield to your lordship in everything.*
>> *Yes* _____
>> *No* _____
>> *Including my eating* _____

31

I must quit being nervous about tomorrow's bread.

DOESN'T OUR BIBLE SAY, "Man shall not live by bread alone"? Straight from the story of Jesus' temptation, "It is written, Man shall not live by bread alone" (Matt. 4:4, KJV).

So give us bread and gravy, bread and honey, bread and jelly, bread and thick cream cheese. And for the likes of us, certain breads on certain occasions can even go it alone. Sourdough bread, raisin bread, banana nut bread, cinnamon bread, date bread, zucchini bread, bread of every ilk. Plus the bread variations. Muffins—bran muffins, blueberry muffins, English muffins. Also buns, biscuits, rolls—rolls too numerous to mention, except maybe we should mention hard rolls. Hard rolls with sesame seeds or, given enough butter, hard rolls without seeds.

Then while pondering rolls, I simply must not be disloyal to my very favorite rolls. These are rolls at their epitome: Martha's Danish pecan rolls.

Danish? Did I hear "Danish"? Now there's a sound we can tune to. Cheese Danish, prune Danish, and what is your favorite Danish? Did you know there is in New York City a Danish delicatessen with more than fifty different kinds of Danish? (Fifty guesses, how do I know?)

On and on we fantasize our bread: Then into our flight of fancy comes this simple phrase from the Lord's Prayer, "Give us this day our daily bread" . . . "the bread of life today" . . . or, as Lamsa has it, "Give us bread for our needs from day to day."

Wherever did we get our ever-so-human tendency to worry far down the road? True, some people come by it out of necessity. With no crops, no job, no future, it would be natural to worry about essentials. But some of us from somewhere picked up another kind of worry. This is the kind which can only be accurately described as chronic concern for non-essentials.

Where is our answer then to this complicated morass of inner tension? Like all problems, for the Christian the answer is in the Book:

My God shall supply all your need (Phil. 4:19, KJV).

Your Father knoweth what things ye have need of (Matt. 6:8, KJV. See also Matt. 6:22 and Luke 12:30).

33

Today he knows and tomorrow he'll know, and on and on he provides the essentials if we trust and obey and live his way.

Moffatt in his translation has a bit more generous rendering: "Give us this day our *bread for the morrow.*" Thank you, Dr. Moffatt. Yet even you offer no carte blanche for those of us with fatty-think:

> *"Twelve more pounds to my ideal weight and then I can eat again."*
>
> *"Three more days on this seven-day diet and then I can celebrate."*

Come now, Charlie, and all fatties everywhere praying the Lord's Prayer, the proper meaning is:

> *Lord, I want to get over this nervousness about my daily bread, and tomorrow's too. I want to trust your promise that you will meet my needs. From day to day make me the kind of eater you can trust.*
>
> *Amen*

All my grudges make me hungry.

"Forgive us our debts, as we forgive our debtors."
Matthew 6:12, KJV

" . . . our trespasses. . . ."
verse 12, Knox

". . . our sins. . . ."
verse 12, TLB

*"Forgive us the wrong we have done, As we have forgiven
those who have wronged us."*
verse 12, NEB

BEFORE THE MOUNTAINS WERE BROUGHT FORTH, our Creator set up certain rules . . . solid, final, no exceptions. And one of the no-exceptions for all his chunkier children goes like this: If we are ever to shape up, when we pray "forgive me" we are to add "as I forgive others."

Why? Because all our grudges eventually make us hungry. Though we stroke the little darlings and treat them as pets, they will not stay little. Almost without our knowing they grow and grow and grow. Then one day, one awful day, they have become roaring lions circling the citadel, growling for food. And we feed them.

Katherine knows. She's learned the hard way. And in this letter she describes to perfection how "forgive me—forgive them" applies to us.

Katherine's letter

For the last ten years I've had a terrible problem with my weight, up and down, up and down, and mostly up.

I am a Christian. I go to church; I am president of the Mother's Club; I teach Sunday school; I sing in the choir. I have a good job, a good husband, and three good children. But I still have this big problem (no pun intended) with my eating and my weight.

Only lately things have been going better and I decided I should write you. Because you reach so many people I thought if I told you my story it might help someone.

This is my story. When I was seventeen, my best friend did something to me which hurt me so bad I simply could not get over it. Her name is Jean, and if I told you all the details, I'm sure you would understand. But one day about six months ago I discovered something.

On this day I was shopping and I saw someone who reminded me of Jean. Naturally, I began thinking back to all those horrible memories, and before I knew it, here I was in the tea room ordering coconut cake, with ice cream of course.

Now I always say a blessing when I sit down to eat. Always. But this time when I said my blessing, it was as if the Lord himself said in a very clear voice, "Katherine, don't be an idiot. You just finished lunch, a nice diet lunch in this very tea room, remember? Thirty minutes ago, and I was proud of you. So here you are about to eat what you don't need to satisfy what you can't satisfy with any amount of coconut cake or ice cream or both. Why don't you settle this ugly old thing? Why don't you forgive and let me put it where it belongs—far, far away. I'm the one who can handle it!"

36

So help me, that is exactly what happened. And what I did next was just what the Lord told me to do. I forgave. I turned the whole thing over to him.

No it wasn't easy, but he never said it would be, did he? As a matter of fact, I even called Jean and had a long talk by phone. I could hardly believe it—she said she had been feeling so bad lately and thinking of me and would I forgive her and could we get together? So we each drove a hundred miles for lunch one Saturday (no coconut cake).

We talked and talked and I shared my feelings, and she shared hers. When I saw that old happening from her viewpoint, for the first time I could see why she acted the way she did. And do you know I really did feel sorry for her? Her life hasn't worked out the way she wanted—nothing like mine—and she's so defeated.

Well, that's about it, only I think I should tell you we've talked several times by phone these past six months and we've gotten together twice. I'm actually growing to love her. I never thought I could say this, but she really is lovable, and, like I say, she's hurting and needs my love.

Now I should close, and since I began with my weight, that's where I want to conclude. I haven't lost all I need to lose, but I am losing steadily. I feel so much better, not just physically, but mentally, and—most important—spiritually.

So this is what I have decided. I have decided something inside you lets go when you let go of your bitterness and resentment and the old grudges.

For me that is a classic letter and I read it often, because I need it. I need to think about it and I need to live by it. For my own appetite's sake, I need to do what Katherine did—forgive!

Here's one more verse now, straight from the Book. It's interesting that this verse immediately follows our Lord's Prayer: "If you forgive others the wrongs they have done,

37

your heavenly Father will also forgive you" (Matt. 6:14, NEB).

One more time, that final sentence from Katherine: "Something inside you lets go when you let go of your bitterness and resentment and the old grudges."

So many temptations everywhere

"Lead us not into temptation."
Matthew 6:13, KJV

PRINCIPLE: WHEN SO MANY BRILLIANT MINDS come to so many brilliant conclusions, I do well to draw my own conclusion.

True, I may not have the background of the super-schooled, yet they haven't had my background either. Nor do they know my mind, my needs, my inspiration. So how can anyone be sure what the Lord will say to me?

Now, isn't that previous paragraph a bit presumptive? The great God of the universe has his stars to set out every night, every day his sun to keep in its track, his worlds to orbit, and the universal computers to attend. With all He has to do, should I expect personal attention?

Incredible! So incredible most of us have felt what one little girl felt on first hearing the Lord's Prayer. What she thought she heard was, "Our Father who art in heaven, how do you know my name?"

How does he? Nobody knows, child, but the Christian believes. The Christian believes because that is exactly what the Bible promises. Exactly.

Jesus came to tell us that our God is a personal God. He does know you and me. For each and every one of us he has personal concern, personal wisdom. So we presume to pray our prayers our way, and as we pray we affirm with the biblical saints, "O God, thou art *my* God!"

Against the background of this theology, I have a little four-word prayer which I pray as I open my Bible. As I prepare for the day's reading, and again as I think back on what I've read, I pray it. This is the prayer: "*Lord, speak to me!*"

Emphasis on the *me!*

Now, flashing back to paragraph one, I especially use that prayer as I come to verses that are hard to understand. It goes well before those passages with many options and divergent renditions. And one place where it goes especially well is when I pray the puzzlers, such as "Lead us not into temptation, but deliver us from evil."

"Let us not be put to the test . . ." (NTBE).

". . . Rescue us from the evil one" (Weymouth).

"Do not subject us to temptation . . . (Goodspeed).

". . . Keep us clear of temptation." (Phillips).

Then from various sources (one jolly professor, a minister friend, participants in some Bible study groups) come these picturesque offerings:

"Tune out the siren voices."

"Help us say no in plenty of time."

"Snatch us from the fire before we get burned."

"Draw us back when we're coming too close."

And my favorite, the "c&m" rendition: "Nudge me, Lord, when I need a nudge."

As I have struggled with "Lead us not into temptation," two other temptation verses come to help me. The first I call my "before temptation" verse: ". . . He is able to give immediate help to any that are tempted" (Heb. 2:18, Williams).

What a promise! Immediately. He will come this minute, right now, ahead of time. This very second he will come to help me wrestle my temptation down. And some of us have learned the hard way that the time to pray for his help *is* before, not after: "Lord, I have the feeling that this is going to be a difficult dinner, an especially attractive spread, a hard season. So as I approach, I want you with me, ahead of time."

My second temptation verse can best be labeled "after temptation": "Happy is the man who remains firm under temptation, for when he has stood the test, he shall have the satisfaction God has promised those who love him all the way" (James 1:12, compiled from various translations).

I like the taste of all those alluring foods, but would they taste as good as the taste of good behavior?

Pride is a negative word for some, but doesn't it come on positive when we know it is genuine pride for genuine courage?

"Thrill" is a misunderstood word too, but is there any thrill quite like the thrill of knowing we are living his way?

There are those who say every temptation withstood makes us stronger. That is one fine idea, but is it true for me? I'm not sure. But I am sure of this: <u>Every temptation withstood makes me realize his way *is* the only way</u>.

If ever there was a fatty's word, this is the word: Temptation. For us every day is temptation day. Monday, Tuesday, Wednesday—every day. Every hour. "Even at 3:00 A.M.," the ad says, "we are baking it just for you. Fluffy white bread, plus cinnamon twists with frosting." Every moment somewhere these pleasant little devils of temptation are up and at it, creating their temptations just for us.

More than fifty times, our Bible leads us to think some thoughts about temptation. A great study, this. Fifty times great, and always it comes out here: <u>"He is our ever-present help in temptation."</u>

Prayer:
Master of power and strength, lead me not into temptation. Rescue me and all my struggling friends. Do not subject us. Keep us clear. Nudge us when we need a nudge.

Amen

THE TWENTY-THIRD PSALM

Like the Lord's Prayer, Psalm 23 is so familiar we only tend to "say" it. But when we tell the Lord we'll mean it this time, he does a nice thing. At any given phrase he may surprise us. It is almost as though he opens some little door and one of those automatic lights comes on: "See! Here it is! This is exactly what you've been looking for. Let's have a good time thinking it through."

I must learn to distinguish between wanting and needing.

Am I faithful enough to my quiet time?

All my fears can make me hungry.

Is my table his table?

I must learn to distinguish between wanting and needing.

"The Lord is my shepherd, I shall not want."
Psalm 23:1, KJV

MARTHA AND I live in hurricane country. For fifteen years we've lived on islands in the Atlantic. Two different islands—each connected to the mainland by five to twenty miles of causeway. At low tide our road looks like many other roads. But at high tide comes that definite ocean feeling.

Dangerous living? Sometimes, during hurricane season. Hurricanes are awesome—devastating if they come our way and deadly for those who will not take them seriously. But there is one advantage to hurricanes. We have at least forty-eight hours warning. The weather advisories keep us posted. "It's headed there, it's headed here. You better leave."

During these fifteen years we've lived on islands several of our friends lost their homes from tornadoes in Nebraska, Arkansas, Texas, Michigan. And from their reports tornadoes have to be worse than hurricanes. No time to batten down the hatches, tape windows, turn off power. No time even to save the precious items.

So if by some quirk of fate we had to choose a climatic horror, we'd vote for the hurricane. With these at least we might save some things.

If you were told to leave home, if you knew this meant your home might not be there when you returned, what would you take? In our fifteen years on islands we've had that hurried choice once. Would you believe we chose our toothbrushes and a change of underwear?

For an exercise in sorting values fast, such an experience can't be beat. One precious thing. Maybe two? Three? What would you take? (We decided next time we'd add that collage of our children's pictures.)

The saints have a term which applies here. They label this kind of sorting out "reducing our multiplicity." That is one fine term for anyone who reads a newspaper, turns on television, opens a magazine, drives past billboards. As one poet says it, "Always the storm of propaganda blows."

Always, it does, and into this kind of world comes the psalmist saying, "The Lord is my shepherd, I shall not want." With a reminder like that, it is small wonder the Twenty-third Psalm rates number one. In almost every survey of favorite Scripture passages, this is the winner.

Some of our feverish wanting does come from "the storm of propaganda." Then in addition there are other breezes inside most of us. Certain of our wanting has long roots. I once asked participants at a retreat to write their thoughts on Psalm 23. They were divided into groups, assigned to particular verses. Here are two statements on verse 1 which helped every one of us in the retreat to track some of our own wants.

Statement one is from a young bride:

When I grew up, I had almost everything any child could want, and if I didn't have it, I asked and they gave it to me. Then we got married and you know how that is. We're living on a budget so I can't have everything, and this is all so new to me, especially the worry. But that's not the worst. The worst is that I seem to be developing a kind of chronic resentment. I do love Johnny, but for the first time I'm beginning to realize how much I love things too, and how much I want them.

Charlie, you must lay firm hold on this little trick of the human mind. If we know we can't have it, we might want it only because we can't have it.
Lord, help me to want what you want.

Statement two is from successful middle-aged manufacturer.

I was brought up poor, and I do mean poor. So I decided when I got through school I was going to get it all. Well, I did get a lot more than most people ever see. You think I'm satisfied? To be perfectly honest, I'm not, and the reason is that the more I get, the more I want. Believe me it's a terrible feeling, this continual state of unhappiness. And I would advise anyone to get hold of it early because if you don't, it goes on re-creating itself. With every new acquisition, you begin thinking what else you want.

Could I be making myself miserable because I have created a situation where the more I get the more I want?
Lord, help me to want what you want.

Question for pensive pondering right here:
In any way does my over-eating have roots in childhood? Back there did I always get what I wanted when I was hungry, even more than I needed?

Or did I not get what I wanted at mealtime, and did that make me want too much?

Answer: The answer of Psalm 23, verse 1.

Philippians 4:19 adds this nice thought: "My God shall supply all your need" (KJV).

For reducing multiplicity at mealtime, this is another good question: If I had to choose a half-dozen foods to meet my needs for an extended period, what would they be?
(eggs, milk, bread, bananas, peas, turkey)

Prayer (again and again):
Lord, help me to want what you want.
                                                    Amen

Am I faithful enough to my quiet time?

> *"He maketh me to lie down in green pastures:*
> *He leadeth me beside still waters.*
> *He restoreth my soul."*
> Psalm 23:2, KJV

MOST OF US have heard numberless speakers on Psalm 23. One of those I remember best was a Basque sheepherder. He came from twenty generations of Iberian shepherds, and this is his description of the shepherd-sheep relationship:

Holy Land sheep exceed in herding instinct. Each takes his place in the grazing line in the morning and keeps the same position throughout the day. Once, however, during the day each sheep leaves its place and goes to the shepherd. Whereupon the shepherd stretches out his hand as the sheep approaches with expectant eyes and mild little baas. The shepherd rubs its nose, scratches its chin, whispers affectionately into its ears. The sheep, meanwhile, rubs against the shepherd's leg, nibbles at his ear, and rubs its cheek against his face. After a few minutes of this communion, the sheep returns to its place in the feeding line.

Almost every Christian would agree that a time of special communion with the Good Shepherd is a must for daily living at its best. And some of us fatties would also agree that the more faithful we are to our quiet time, the better our self-control.

When in our quiet time we tune to the Inner Presence, he does have a way of leading us to the stillness. Somehow he senses our sensitivity, and as our day moves along, he leads us to other moments for being restored. Our Lord is the Lord of time-gaps for restoring. He restoreth our soul, our strength, our perspective, our ability to evaluate. Plus this big plus: When we let him, he restores our self-control for right eating.

Common questions on the quiet time include, "What part of the day is best?" and "When could I ever find time?" To which come the same simple answers. Any time is the best time, and nobody ever finds time. Time for quiet has to be made.

One of our friends says her best time is late at night when everyone else is in bed.

A successful executive we know says his quiet time is right after lunch. He closes his door, disconnects his phone and heads for the green pastures, the still waters, and the restoral of his soul.

For me the day goes best with an early quiet time. I once went through my Bible for every "early in the morning" reference, and it was an especially profitable study. But say it again, the key word is not *when*. The key word is *whether*. Whether we do or do not create time for the Good Shepherd can make a mighty difference. It can make all the difference in long-range right eating, long-term appetite management, long years of weight control.

That short phrase, "He restoreth my soul," takes an interesting turn with certain scholars. They insist it should be rendered, "He turneth back my soul." All of us struggling with temptation to eat the wrong things can understand that. Shades of the Lord's Prayer: "Nudge me, turn me back when I'm moving toward temptation."

Conclusion: Whether we spend our quiet time studying the Bible, reading from the devotional classics, praying, or simply being absolutely still in his Presence, this has to be true:

> *Whatever time we choose*
> *and all the time we give*
> *by any method,*
> *time for those green pastures,*
> *still waters,*
> *restoral of soul*
> *is must time for any sheep*
> *of the Good Shepherd*
> *and especially*
> *for the heavier sheep*
> *like us.*

All my fears can make me hungry.

"I will fear no evil: for thou art with me."
Psalm 23:4, KJV

GRANDMA NIMROD taught me a good thing that day of the funeral. We had buried one of her distant relatives and now the crowd gathered for what by any other name was time at the feeding trough.

The table was loaded with great stacks of sandwich makings and snacks of every kind. There were cakes, pies, desserts— crying out for attention. And all the good ladies of my parish were urging their pastor's special attention to each one's special offering. So, as per my usual custom, I set out to accommodate.

Now with plate heaped high I looked for a spot to consume my takings, and over by the window sat Grandma Nimrod. I had seen her on occasion although, being very old and very fragile, she was not a Sunday regular. Yet each time I had sensed in her an aura of peace, an inner oneness. Now began a pleasant chat, a solid visit while I ate and ate and ate.

After the usual weather talk, the "how are you"'s, our conversation suddenly took a different turn. With some probing questions we moved to classified data. Forty years later I still remember exactly what she asked, exactly what I answered, exactly the sage advice she gave me.

"You're worried, son, aren't you? Something troubling you?" (I have often wondered how much she knew about gourmandizing and inner stress. Did my overburdened plate clue her in? Or did she simply know that very young pastors sometimes need very old grandmas?)

"You're right, Grandma, I am worried. Something is troubling me." Then I took out my little black book with memo pads, "See these things I have to do. Committees, planning, following through, all these matters I must attend. People waiting to see me, wanting something. This is a big church, Grandma. Maybe too big for a pastor so young. How will I ever satisfy everyone?"

It's exciting how the Lord leads us sometimes to certain benedictions we'll be needing through the years. That's what her words were now, one of my all time special benedictions.

"Are you doing the best you can?"

"I think so."

"Then listen to me. I think you're too worried what people think. Take it from an old grandma. When you're doing the best you can, God doesn't judge you anywhere near as hard as people judge you—not if you're doing your best."

Early in life most of our fears do tend to be people-fears. What will they say, think, do? How will they like me, receive me, react to me?

Then as we mature and gain confidence, our people-fears may ebb a bit. Does it matter now what "they" think? So, our worries are over? Indeed not. Haven't they just begun?

Now come the real concerns. Health, old age, and what is this pain I feel? Last week another friend died. Heart attack. Then there is the economy. How ever will our dollars stretch? Monsters all, these worries shiver us through and through.

What does this have to do with pounds and diets and over-eating? For some of us the answer is that fears and appetite are channeled on the same circuit. Little fears, big fears, and all the fears in-between turn on our hunger and needle our wants.

I have one friend who, when even slightly anxious, loses her appetite. Completely. When the winds of worry come, they carry off her hunger. For forty-plus years she's been like that. And why do the very same winds turn me to the pantry, the candy box, the refrigerator?

Answer: Nobody knows all the answers to our inner goings on. But do we need to know? If he knows, and we know him, this is the answer of answers: "I will fear no evil: for thou art with me."

Is my table his table?

"Thou preparest a table before me."
Psalm 23:5, KJV

IF YOU HAVE TRAVELED much in Mexico, you have heard this lovely phrase: "Mi casa, su casa"—"My house is your house."

They say it when they invite you, as you enter their door, before you sit down. Good. But there is another nice addition you would hear if you were invited to one home we know.

These are special Latin American friends—warm and loving—and as we make our way to their dining room, we hear, "My table is your table."

Do you have certain phrases which seem to rendezvous in your heart until they have gathered their thoughts to do you good? This is one such phrase for me: "My table is your table."

Tables are top billing for the likes of us—kitchen tables, dining tables, coffee tables (with hors d'oeuvres), restaurant tables, big tables, small tables, high tables, low tables. But for us fatties, there is always the same question: "Is our table the Lord's table?"

Here we are at Psalm 23, a little more than halfway through, and the psalmist would bring up tables.

"Thou preparest a table before me!"

Quaint touch. Nice sound. Comforting. Or is it? Could this be the very stuff of which, three times each day our lives shape up?

Like most of the Shepherd's Psalm, these few words have many interpretations. One of my favorites is that which says the reference is to "table land," a high place in the terrain. Up here the shepherd could go himself for a long view. Up here he could see where they had been, where they were going, where they needed to change directions. He could spot water, locate the smoother road, the valley of shadow.

He could also see the enemy up here and in emergencies he could call up the flock for safety. Of course, there would be some sheep who wouldn't listen, wouldn't come.

Take a bow, Charlie. How many times have you heard the Good Shepherd calling you up and you wouldn't go?

Lord, I'm sorry. By the loving hands of this woman thou gavest me thou preparest a table before me. She knows what I need and how much. She knows what does me good. Salads, fowl, lean meat, fish, fruits, and all attractively done. Happy colors, happy talk, happy memories.

Yet how many times have I gone from her table, your table, to the cookie jar, the malt shop, or to a box of crispy crackers. Great God, forgive me. I do want to be one of the good sheep of the Good Shepherd. Trusting. Obedient. Responding today to the upward call.

So one more time I pray, and one more time I mean it:

> *Every time I sit to eat this day may it be so—"My house is your house, my table, your table!"*
>
> *Amen*

THE TEN COMMANDMENTS

I don't like the Ten Commandments. Or shouldn't I say I'm not always wild about them when they apply especially to me? (Certainly, I think they're great applied to other people. I wouldn't like anyone stealing my things, and who in right mind would approve killing?)

Yet any true believer knows the Ten Commandments are solid rock. We do not break these rules, and if we try we only break ourselves. That's how God set it up, and how he put us together.

Interesting, too, how pointed the Ten Commandments can be—pointed straight at our extra poundage.

I will put God first.
I mean I will try to put God first.

I will try to think straight about my parents.

I will lay a firm hand on jealousy.

I will put God first.
I mean I will try to put God first.

"Thou shalt have no other gods before me."
Exodus 20:3, KJV

(For another rendition of
the Ten Commandments, see Deuteronomy 5)

NOTHING, NO ONE, NO OTHER GODS are to take precedence
over the Lord of the Ten Commandments. That's what it
says, and this is an awesome charge. He will never be satisfied
with anything other than first place.

Now that is a verse for the over-eater!

What if I don't put him first? Then I am breaking the
first commandment. And when they asked Jesus, "Which is
the great commandment?" (Matt. 22:36, KJV—"The most
important," Norlie), Jesus said that "the great and first com-

mandment" (v. 38, ASV—"the foremost," Weymouth) is, "Thou shalt love the Lord thy God with all thy heart, and with all thy soul, and with all thy mind, and with all thy strength" (v. 37, NEB).

One of my favorite proud-parent stories is from a father and mother who were devout Christians and wanted their children to know the Lord too. They were especially good at techniques for stimulating family conversation about spiritual things.

One such technique was their Sunday practice of discussing the sermon on their way home from church. Since they lived some distance away, there would be plenty of time for thorough consideration.

On this day the minister (a friend of the whole family) had preached from Jesus' great commandment, "Thou shalt love the Lord thy God with all thy heart, and with all thy soul, and with all thy mind, and with all thy strength." As they thought about this together, nine-year-old Timothy summed the entire thing up with, "He didn't miss anything, did he?"

He didn't.

Neither did he leave us to wonder what might happen if we really would live with no other gods. What would happen? All kinds of good things, said Jesus, including a greater sensitivity to the blessings as they arrive. Big blessings, little blessings, and so many blessings often overlooked.

We have many songbirds making their home on our island. Some days when they come to the feeder and sing their praise to the Lord, I get this mysterious feeling they are singing just for me!

It's a fine feeling, very fine! But mysterious? Why should it be mysterious? Isn't this exactly what our Lord promised? If we try to put him first and keep on trying, all things will be added, and even the singing of the birds will have special meaning just for us.

> *Prayer:*
>
> *Thank you, Lord, for each of your Ten Commandments, and especially for this one.*
>
> *Thank you too for explaining it so well with your call on all my heart, all my soul, all my mind, all my strength.*
>
> *This day I will try <u>again</u> to have no other gods before me.*
>
> *Amen*

I will try to think straight about my parents.

"Honour thy father and thy mother."
Exodus 20:12, KJV

SHE WAS A BEAUTIFUL YOUNG WOMAN under all those pounds. The west Oklahoma breeze had colored her cheeks with a permanent glow, and I liked what I saw in her cheeks. But oh, the rest of Mary Ann!

Lonely now, she came for counseling. She had been rejected too often by too many, she said, and she knew the reasons. Every morning there they were (the reasons) on her scale. Too, too many pounds.

Why would she come to me? Why not? As anyone could plainly see, I'd know a thing or two about pounds and what they can do to self-esteem, and heavy things like that.

It didn't take long until we were well into her problem. Every night after work she would stop at a dairy that had superb ice creams of every kind. They also had gleaming white tables. In their nice little alcove you could sit and watch the evening traffic making its way home. Trains going by too. You could order a huge sundae. And then?

"Then," said Mary Ann, "I sit there and think about men. About the men I wish I could go with, the men at work, the ones I'd love to have married. But mostly I think about my father."

On from there she went with the sad dirge of her inner father-loneliness. The distant dad, the aloof dad, the dad she would like to have known.

You must have heard the story countless times, "Little girl longing to know stranger." Fat Mary Ann could have written the script.

Is it mere coincidence that most of the fatties I know have had a distorted father relationship?*

---

* My book, *The Fat Is in Your Head* (Waco, TX: Word Books, 1972), deals at length with obesity and mother memories. Those whose parent problems tip to the matronly side may find that writing helpful (pp. 60–80). Since the publication of that book, I have heard from numerous fellow-strugglers asking, "Why so much on mother? My problem, I think, may be my father thoughts. Let's have a word about that."
Very good idea! Let's do it.

Reports from a discussion group on "My Father and My Weight":

My dad wasn't aloof. He watched me like a hawk. He didn't want me fat, so he checked every bite I took, and it made me so nervous I think it even made me hungry.

My problem was the opposite. Papa was fat. Very fat. So I ate with him—all that candy and rich food. I can remember yet how he would cuddle me when I was little and we'd lick our suckers while we watched TV. I really loved papa and I nearly died inside when he died. All those wonderful memories, they still get to me.

Our father was a tyrant. He demanded perfection and that's what he got from my sisters and my brother and me. But do you think he was ever satisfied? No way. The more we performed to his standard, the more he wanted. You probably know what happened. Some of us said, "Forget it," and some of us did crazy things, and my mother, she almost became a basket case. Me? Well, I guess you can see what happened to me. I tried to eat my way out of it.

Enough of this prodigious parade. The fat fact stands. Some of the pounds we carry had their start way back there. All our influences were not holy. Not "Holy" in the sense of its original meaning, which is "wholeness."

So what can we do now? Today what steps can we take?

1. *We can face facts*, surface the truth, tell it like it is. With friend, confidant, counselor, or alone we must look

in the hidden nooks and not be afraid. By no arrangement of this fourth commandment, no twist of the original language, are we expected to honor what is not honorable. So wherever our parents were honorable, we should give honor, but we should not burn incense. Until we understand this thoroughly, and sort it out, we may go on eating to satisfy longings which can never be satisfied with food.

2. *We can forgive.* Most of our parents did the best they could with their background, their inner struggles, their inability to understand their problems—including the problems they had with us. Let us have mercy.

3. *We can teach ourselves to contrast.* As children we were taught to pray, "Our Father who art in heaven." In church and from our children's books we learned of the heavenly Father. Unfortunately too we learned all this before we were able to contrast. At this young age we could only compare: "God is like my father? . . . My father is too busy . . . my father has no time for me . . . my father is not nice to my mother. . . . God is like this? . . . Maybe I wouldn't even like God!"

Nomination for another of the heavy's heavy challenges: to *face* parental negatives, to *forgive* parental negatives, to *contrast* parental negatives with the loving heavenly Father whom Jesus came to reveal.

All important understanding: In whatever ways my parents were not what they should have been, I must comprehend this—God is the very opposite. In whatever ways they were loving, were perfectly wise—that is what God is like.

When I do these three things—

Face facts
Forgive
Contrast—

I may set my foot on solid ground to a much more solid me.

For further meditation:

Jesus said, "Whoever comes to me cannot be my disciple unless he loves me more than he loves his father and his mother, his wife and his children, his brothers and his sisters, and himself as well" (Luke 14:26, TEV).

I will lay a firm hand on my jealousy.

> *"Thou shalt not covet."*
> *Exodus 20:17,* KJV

> *(For some New Testament thoughts on this theme, see Romans 7:7–8.)*

SHELDON IS MY SKINNY FRIEND. He can eat and eat and eat, which is exactly what he does when we break bread together. First, a creamy chowder. Then salad heavy with blue cheese and croutons. Add french fries with fried chicken. Finalize with German chocolate cake. Ah, Sheldon, to be like you.

I read in our newspaper last week of a man who killed because he long had coveted what was not his. Nothing new, really. Coveting can devastate. Or it can be the milder kind which destroys slowly. Slowly it eats away at us, causing us to overeat.

Item: *It isn't always what I eat. Sometimes it's what's eating on me that makes me eat.*

When we have studied the biblical word *covet* in its various shades of meaning, we do come within the shadow of our more common words—*envy* and *jealousy*. Yet however we spell it, the meaning remains. This is one more commandment calling for serious attention.

We have a mouse in our house right now, and we don't like mice around here. We have never seen him/her, but by the usual signs we know the little demon is living it up on us. Marsh mice are like that. Here along the coast if we don't keep at them, they can be a pestilence. They're very sly and, for a long time, they get by. But we'll get him. One day he'll turn careless and bang goes another bother. As any experienced householder knows, if we didn't stay with it, keep resetting traps with fresh cheese, we'd soon be overrun with marsh mice.

Jealousy is so much like the marsh mice. It lives in the dark, runs around all over the place—daring. Most of the time we don't even know it's there. But then there are signs. A nervous kind of feeling, a bit of guilt maybe. And there's one more thing. Almost without our knowing, jealousy attacks our system at its most vulnerable point: appetite.

Tell me, Moses, up there on the mountain, didn't you and the Lord talk about many things? How could ten commandments cover all the sins of humankind forever? If we could know how you sorted out, deleted, added to, that would be a story. But did you tack on this tenth commandment as a trailer? Stealing, killing, adultery—these are such monsters compared to bearing false witness, remembering the Sabbath day, coveting. Or are they? Do the little things*really trigger the big things?

Test on Commandment Ten

1. Jealousy is not one of my problems. Yes _____ No _____ Never has been _____ Maybe _____

2. (For those who answer "yes" to question one)
   A. The person I most envy is_____.
   B. The types I tend to covet are_____.
   C. The things which other people have and I want are
   _____.
   D. My most vivid memory of a jealous time in my life (some incident, or lengthy struggle) is _____
   _____ .
   E. I have long ago surrendered all my envies, my jealousies, my coveting to the Lord. Yes _____ No _____

3. I do _____, do not _____ think this commandment could in any way affect my appetite.

---

* For added meditation on the small negatives see "The Little Foxes" on p. 165.

Prayer:

Lord, you painted with such a wide brush that time on the mountain with Moses. I do want to live by your commandments. I do believe they lead to health and long life and peace in the heart.

Yet something tends to make me hungry. By your standards, this day I want to be honest in every way, including, "Thou shalt not covet."

Amen

DANIEL—WHERE HAVE ALL THE HEROES GONE?

An editorial writer says he grew up with stars in his eyes. There were many big names to admire, and even in his hometown there were good, solid characters to reverence.

So what happened? "Where have all the heroes gone?" he asks. "Is no one left for admiration?"

I hope the man was only overstating, but whether he was or wasn't, I do wish he knew Moses, David, Amos, Hosea, Peter, Andrew, Luke—and especially Daniel!

Have I really made up my mind?

Would I think better if I ate less?

Am I letting others direct my eating?

Do I eat too much away from home?

Have I really made up my mind?

*"Daniel was most anxious not to
defile himself with food."*
Daniel 1:8, JB

"Daniel purposed in his heart . . ."
v. 8, KJV

*"Daniel determined not to contaminate
himself by touching the food and wine assigned to him."*
v. 8, NEB

*"Daniel resolved that he would not
defile himself with the king's rich food."*
v. 8, RSV

"Daniel made up his mind."
v. 8, TEV

DANIEL HAD AN EATING PROBLEM. Straight from the Word
of the Lord we know he did. True, it was not our particular
kind of problem, yet it certainly was a problem.

I like the way Daniel handled his problem. I like his style,
his courage, his grace under fire. And here's a plus: he gives
me that very important feeling, "I did it. You can do it!"

Was he fat? Probably not, but the opening chapters of
his book tell us that he had plenty of opportunity to eat
and eat and eat. The gastronomically supreme, the very best,
the tastiest—it was all there for his having.

Daniel was a victim of that unfortunate practice of his time whereby a foreign king who successfully invaded a country would carry off the choice people. He would take them back to his own land where he would train them, reshape them, or do whatever he wished with them. They were part of the conqueror's spoils.

When Daniel and his friends arrived in their new setting, "The king assigned them a portion of the rich food which the king ate" (v. 5). We can assume that the king's chef would rank with the best. He would know how to plan, how to prepare, how to produce the finest of gourmet foods. So here is our friend Daniel, exactly where we've been ten thousand times: tempted to gourmandize ad infinitum, ad too too much, ad pounds.

Then into the story, verse 8, come five words for our attention: *"Daniel made up his mind."*

We are not told *when* Daniel made up his mind, but we can be sure he must have begun making it up years before. Most commitment *does* begin way back in our histories because ordinarily the resolve which sticks has long, long roots.

Here is that question for us fatties again: Have we, once for all, taken the pledge?

Diets are important. So is a wide knowledge of the body, of foods, of nutrition. But does anything matter more than to decide with no equivocation, "Lord, I *will* be true!!"?

This much I know. The king's chef could not have been more expert than my queen of the culinary arts. There is none better. None. So you can see I do understand you, Daniel, and I thank you for your reminder. If we wait till we arrive at the table, it's too late and our resolve is long gone. Sometime, somewhere in advance we must make up our minds.

Yet for the Christian this isn't exactly what it appears on the surface, is it? Germane to our faith is the startling fact that we *cannot* win the battle on our own. Only after we've accepted that shocker does this bit of Good News come: We don't need to do it on our own! Our Lord will help us if we let him (emphasis on the "let"). "Let this mind be in you which was also in Christ Jesus" (Phil. 2:5).

Prayer:

Lord Jesus, thank you for being a thinking Lord; thinking in me, for me, through me, when I let you.

Thank you too for the great gift of letting me make up my own mind. Right now, this minute, forever I yield this mind and all its thought patterns for your thoughts, your patterns. Take my mind and let it be consecrated, Lord, to thee.

Amen

Would I think better if I ate less?

*"So the steward took away their rich food. . . .
and in every matter of wisdom and
understanding . . . he found them ten times better."*
Daniel 1:16, 20 RSV

SUPER THINK" is an interesting term of the pop psychologists, and we've all had our times of "super think." At such times our minds are extra sharp. Problems unravel, answers come clear, and we can almost *feel* our brains working. For the Christian this is an exciting sensation, because it is one more indicator that we are in tune with the divine mind.

For some of us, "super think" and right eating have a direct relationship. On those days of appetite obedience we can probe deeper, see farther, sort out, cut through, organize, rearrange, understand better, gain new insights. And why? For the Christian fatty there is only one answer: Away at the center of our minds we are in touch with a wisdom far greater than our own. Because we have been obedient, our Lord can think his thoughts through us.

This link between food intake and mental clarity is as ancient as the Old Testament. Any fellow struggler pondering the book of Daniel will hear the message. How we think and how we eat *are* closely interwoven.

Daniel and his friends were "handsome and skillful . . . endowed with knowledge . . . and competent to serve in the king's palace."

But now comes a conflict. The king had given his caretaker of the captives specific directions. Spare nothing, instruct these boys in the ways of the court, and school them in the language. In every way they were to have the best, including the best food.

Exact diet? We do not know, but we do know this: "Best" meant something different to Daniel than it had ever meant to the king.

So Daniel made Ashpenaz (the caretaker) this proposition. "Test us for ten days. Give us vegetables to eat and water to drink. Then compare us with the young men who are eating the food of the royal court. At the end of that time look us over carefully. Base your decision on our appearance."

Sounds reasonable. But to Ashpenaz there was another consideration. The king had decided how Daniel and his friends must look. And if they did not meet these expectations, wouldn't this endanger the caretaker's future? Certainly it would (v. 10). Yet Daniel was persuasive and his request was granted. "God gave Daniel favor . . . in the sight of [Ashpenaz]" (v. 9).

Happy ending. When their time was up, they did look healthier, fitter, stronger than those who were eating the royal food. "In *every* matter of wisdom and understanding concerning which the king inquired of them, he found them ten times better than all the magicians and enchanters that were in all his kingdom" (v. 20).

One great story.

One inescapable conclusion: *Eat right. Think right.*

While we are in the mood for thinking right, comes now a side item. Some translators say Daniel and his friends were "better in appearance and 'fatter' in flesh." "Fatter?" No problem with that word if we return to the original. Some terms are almost impossible to accurately interpret in our language and this is one. The original Old Testament word for "fat" is our word "fitter."

Another interesting note: Daniel and his friends asked for and were granted "vegetables with water" (v. 12). We have some vegetarian friends who eat no meat, no food products whatsoever that are not vegetable-based. We've eaten at their table several times and it never ceases to surprise us how many different dishes they come up with. Good eating. Delicious. And our friends *look* good, "fit" in every way.

Today, remembering Daniel, I will give some thought to these questions:

How "fit" am I by my own definition of fitness?

How "fit" do I look? To myself? To others?

And to arrive at some honest answers to those questions I will give serious consideration to these checkpoints:

1. I do feel better, think sharper when I eat what I know is right. Yes _____ No _____

2. When I have been eating exactly what I believe the Lord wants, I look better to myself. Yes _____ No _____

3. During these periods when I am living his way in my diet, there really is a special feeling in my soul. Yes _____ No _____

Prayer:

Thank you, Lord, for a body which responds right to what is right. Thank you too for a mind which works as you meant it to work when I eat like you meant me to eat.

And thank you for this great story from Daniel. Write it on my heart that I too may have the courage to live your way.

Amen

Am I letting others direct my eating?

> *"The king assigned them a daily portion of the rich food which the king ate and of the wine which he drank."*
> Daniel 1:5, RSV

RICH! BEAUTIFUL WORD. Straight from one of our dictionaries: "Sumptuous, containing plenty of butter, eggs, flavoring, et cetera." And on the wings of that *et cetera* our minds take off.

Comfort me with the rich and the creamy. Cheese cake, chocolate pudding, lemon meringue pie, butterscotch souffle, ice cream, whipped cream, coffee cream, strawberries with cream, bananas in cream—almost anything in cream.

Breathes there a fatty with hunger so dead he never to

himself has said, "Oh to be first in line at the heavenly smorgas-bord" (see p. 29). Substitute "she" for "he" and let the ladies in. All of us together long to hear the good word: "This is heaven. Eat and eat and eat. Feed your happy selves on the king's rich foods."

What did Daniel do? Or shouldn't I be asking what would I have done? Alack and alas, as my British friends say, I think I know the answer. One of our cohorts, a very funny lady, calls the procedure "pigging out."

How many times have we "pigged out," and how often at the slightest urging? Urgings from inside, urgings with mother echoes, urgings from everywhere. "But I baked it just for you!" . . . "You can diet tomorrow." . . . "Second help-ings are free." These we have always with us, urgings of every variety, including that true jewel of a friend who says, "You know what I think? I think you're looking much too thin. You're wasting away. How do you know you're not overdoing?"

And Daniel, was there ever an excuse like yours? "The king prefers his servants plump. You must not anger the king."

Brave Daniel. Strong Daniel. Hard-to-believe Daniel. Daniel the Great!

"Daniel the Great" is no exaggeration. When the rich foods are jumping up and down, calling our name, when we're urged by many voices to dive right in, it does require real greatness to tune out the sirens and pray, "Lord, what do you want?"

Prayer:
Heavenly Father, you made me. You know
I want to eat every bite of every one of the

83

rich foods. I love rich foods, but even more I do love You. Today I want to eat for You. Tell me what to say to the king, the friend, the man, the nice lady, the people, anyone anywhere nudging me away from my commitment.

Right now I affirm it again: Most of all I want to be all yours.

Amen

Do I eat too much away from home?

"Nebuchadnezzar, King of Babylon,
attacked Jerusalem, and captured the people.
Then he selected from among the exiles
certain promising young men. These he would
train for service in the royal court.
And among them was Daniel."
(synopsis of Daniel 1:1–6)

Do you TEND TO OVEREAT away from your own address? Traveling, strange places, strange faces, surroundings unfamiliar—how do you do then? Most of the over-ample I know have a special repertoire of excuses for those times away from home. And unless we set up special guards for these times, we may find ourselves stuffing it in, not because we're hungry, but because we're lonesome.

All of us who travel by air surely have had this experience. We arrive at the airport early. Then, after checking our bags, we ask that all-important question, "Do we eat on this flight?" . . . "Negative. Insufficient time."

Everyone knows it is never wise to fly without eating. So we hunt up the snack bar or the cafeteria and eat. Then after takeoff comes the big, wonderful surprise. They *do* serve a meal on this flight. Praises be, the agent misread what it said. Let us break bread together.

After all, we paid for this. Why not? So here we sit, eating, not because we need it (we've already eaten), but because it's there. And as any frequent flying fatty knows, we even eat when it's not worth eating!

Why ever do we behave like this? One answer may be that we left our resolve back where we came from. Commitment *is* a private matter and our own locale *is* the place for private things. Out in the world, high in the sky, with no one to watch—no commitment.

But here comes Daniel with something to say about how to eat away from home. Or actually the message today is more appropriately titled, "How *not* to eat away from home."

We can be sure that Daniel was hungry, or at least hungry for something other than transit food. And Daniel was lonesome—far from his homeland, in a strange country, his future unknown, "a stranger in a strange land."

But Daniel determined in his heart that he would not eat of the king's dainties (v. 8).

I think it is fair for you to know when Daniel first became my special friend with so much to say about my eating.

It was at the Pioneer Grill in a small Oklahoma city. The Pioneer Grill was especially known for its breakfast buffet.

Bacon, sausage, ham, scrambled eggs, grits, fried potatoes, home-made biscuits, huge pancakes, waffles for the waffle eaters, syrups of every kind. Then fruit—great bowls of fruit. And their motto? On a beautiful sign it hung over the counter: "Eat up! Come back again and again!"

We met there every Wednesday morning. This was our men's Bible Study—small group, close friends.

So here we sat stuffing it in, devouring our way through the Old Testament. Then came Daniel. Here in this fantasmagoria of food, we studied Daniel for several weeks. Daniel eating for the Lord, Daniel at the king's table, Daniel away from home, Daniel facing the rich foods. And that was when Daniel really became my friend. My inspiring friend.

Prayer:
Heavenly Father, I want to be more like Daniel.

Amen

"OVER-SAY"

Over-Say *is the psychological term for talking too much, for telling more than needs to be told, for blathering on when silence would be better.*

It would be good if certain human tendencies were utterly wiped out at the time of our conversion. But some of these demons do not go away just because we turn to follow a new Leader. Fact is, they might even multiply. That being true, we do well to pray with the Old Testament and New:

"Set a watch, O Lord, before my mouth; keep the door of my lips" (Ps. 141:3–4, KJV).

"Let the word of Christ dwell in me richly in all wisdom" (Col. 3:16, KJV).

Entrance and exit

Am I boring people with my problem?

Do I tend sometimes to over-listen?

What comes out of the mouth
is important too.

*"It is not what goes into a person's
mouth that makes him . . . unclean; rather,
what comes out of it makes him unclean."*
Matthew 15:11, TEV

THIS UNUSUAL STATEMENT of Jesus is the reverse of what
we usually mean when we talk about our weight. Initially
our thoughts are all on intake, tasting, eating, devouring. Intake is an important consideration, because excessive consump-
tion does keep us from shaping up.

Now in Matthew 15:11 the Lord of human behavior is
telling us we must guard what comes out of our mouth too.
Does he mean we should watch what we *say* about what
we eat? Probably. But mining this verse in depth produces
another meaning.

The *quality* of our talk is important.

What we say to people, what we say *about* them, *how* we say what we say—spirit, inflection, tone—these all make a difference.

Then what about *quantity* of talk?

Couldn't that "what" of today's verse rightly be expanded to include "how *much* comes out?"

Such an all-inclusive statement here:

It is not what goes into a person's mouth that makes him . . . unclean; rather, what comes out of it makes him unclean.

plus, how much!

As I hold my conversational pattern up to the searching light of all this could mean, shouldn't I be quiet now?

Prayer:

Lord, I want to be clean. Clean of mind, clean of heart, clean of wrong desires, clean of conversational wrongs.

I do believe my inner condition makes a difference in every way, including the way I eat.

I want to think right, speak right, eat right, because I am right inside with you.

Amen

Am I boring people with my problem?

"Speak no more . . . of this."
Deuteronomy 3:26, RSV

WARNING!

Overweight people trying to do something about their weight are usually bores. They talk about their diets, complain about their diets, brag about their diets. And on and on and on . . . and why don't they go away?

Epitaph from a country tombstone:

> She was a bore
> Much to my sorrow.
> She was here today
> And here tomorrow.

Change "she" to "he" and who doesn't know at least one of the poet's people. But the question for today is, "Am I too among the 'yawners'?"

"Over-say" is a chic psychological label for the quaint term "motor mouth." And didn't we all grow up with something similar? Haven't we all heard, "Count to ten." . . . "Zipper your lip." . . . "Sleep on it."?

Every parent has said it, thought it, shouted it, screamed it: "Not one more word out of you." "That's enough." "Hush." "Be quiet." "Shut up."

Today's verse is one of those innocent little phrases which we could easily overlook. But if we pray "Teach me from the small things too," it may have a real lesson for us.

Apparently Moses had been talking too much, and God now had enough of the great man's badgering. Question: Does the Lord weary of my whining? All our cajoling, advising, complaining does seem a bit much.

Right now Moses is asking, "Why?" He has brought the Lord up to date on his forty year's achievement and now this. He cannot enter the Promised Land. He can look, *yes*, but enter, *no*.

Agitate, agitate, fuss, fuss, fuss. "This isn't fair, Lord! Don't you remember how hard I've worked, how much I've sacrificed, all those times when. . . ?" Then, in the midst of this harangue, the message comes, "Speak no more of this." Which being interpreted means, "Your options have now expired."

It doesn't seem fair. Is there anyone of us who would consider that a square deal? Forty years of service, forty years of trudging is a long time. It's also a long time for dieting, watching the scale go up and down, agonizing. Then one day to hear, "You'll never make your Promised Land." We don't like that, Lord.

So what if we don't like it? What if we do go on fussing?

One answer is "hunger." Ponderous word for ponderous people: "You keep on talking, you'll go on an eating binge!"

Hear ye, hear ye, Charlie! Hear ye all ye fellow strugglers. It is one great day when we make friends inside with this inevitable dictum: We will never, never, never enter the hoped-for country where we can eat all we want and not get fat. Then it is even a greater day when we pray and mean it, "Lord, I don't understand, but I do accept. Amen. Amen, Lord, in its fullest meaning, 'so be it.' "

If we were to pray that prayer until our psychic inner complainers got the message, what would happen around here?

Wouldn't we become more attractive to ourselves? Wouldn't we be less boring to the people around us? Would we be nicer even to God?

Flashing back now to our opening statement, here comes the hard truth again: All overeaters tend to be mouthy. A flood of words from a trickle of thought, that's us. Why? As we have seen, for heavies like us too much mouth in any way is one more indicator of spiritual *dis*-relationship. We have not let the Lord Jesus take control far down at soul center.

If we had, we would know that others are not as interested as we might think in what we've been doing, or how well we've been doing, or in any of our woes. They want to give us a report from *their* interior. Our ministry then is to listen.

Jesus said, "Come unto me," and after that he did not say, "Go recite to the world how much you hurt. Give them some of your favorite 'isn't-it-awful's. Or brag a little. Tell them how well you've done."

Ridiculous. And why? Because that kind of thinking is the very opposite of Christ-like caring. The Lord needs us to quit our moaning and groaning, our bragging or boring; to love as he loved.

Test for progress: Am I increasingly alert to my own over-say? Is there a growing awareness in me that my chief call is not to be ministered unto, but to minister?

Prayer:
Lord, am I also among the boring? Help me to grow in Christ-like concern, to really care about other people and to care more about caring for them as you would care.

Amen

Do I tend sometimes to over-listen?

"Take heed therefore how ye hear."
Luke 8:18 KJV

"So be careful in what frame of
mind you listen."
v. 18, Rieu

"Be careful what you listen to."
v. 18, C&M

FRIEND ONE:
"You're gaining weight, aren't you?"
FRIEND TWO:
"Sure you're not losing too fast?"

FIRST EXPERT:
"Breakfast is the most important meal.
Eat a big breakfast."

SECOND EXPERT:
"You can skip breakfast.
With your day ahead, you'll never miss it."

THESE FOLKS:
"The only way to go is vegetarian."
THOSE FOLKS:
"Eat plenty of beef. You need protein."

AND FROM THE DOCTORS:
"Eat five small meals every day.
Keeps your stomach busy."

"Limit yourself to two meals per day.
It's the only way."

"Fasting is the supreme answer."

"Fasting is dangerous."

"Cut out the eggs.
Cholesterol can kill you."

"The cholesterol scare is ridiculous.
Eggs are an absolute must."

So go the voices—multifarious voices, voices with authentic sound. Then here among the many sounds comes the word of the Lord: "Be careful what you listen to."

So over-say has another facet. We've already heard, "Don't talk too much. Guard your lips." Now comes Jesus in today's verse. "You must also set a watch before your ears."

Paul, as though he knows we might be puzzled by this turn of thought, has some help for us in Colossians 2:8. At first what the apostle says may seem somewhat of a ramble. But on second reading or third, we pick up something similar to Jesus' thoughts on over-listening: "Be careful of high-sounding nonsense" (Phillips); "Beware . . . specious make-believe" (Moffatt). And then, as though carried away with his adjuring, he goes all out in verse 16: "Let no one act as your judge in regard to food and drink" (NAS).

To which any thinking fatty quite rightfully asks, "Did you really mean *no* one, Paul?"

Probably not. We all make sweeping statements on occasion to carry important points. But whether he meant it as said or wants us to temper his words, this I know: Some of my doctors have judged my eating and their thoughts have been exactly what I needed.

I also listen to my favorite cook. (When I'm thinking straight, I do.) Why? Because she's an expert on food. She's trained herself in calories and nutrition, in what foods will do to me, in what I can and can't eat.

Why shouldn't I listen to her too? She loves me. She says she wants me around a long time, and to hear her say that is one of my genuine pleasures.

So? So no doubt about it, I need to pray,

> *Lord, I want to take heed how I hear. I want to be careful in what frame of mind I listen, and also careful what I listen to.*
> *So Lord, help me to listen for your voice.*

*Tune me in to the words of your love—words
I like, and those I do not like but need.*

*And Lord, teach me to tune out those words
which aren't for me. You be my Inner Listener.*

Amen

WHEN I'M DISCOURAGED

"Behold, and see if there be any sorrow like unto my sorrow"
(*Lam. 1:12*, KJV).
Wherein we look at the devastating heaviness of the heavy's woe—
and how it destroys our resolve,
and what it can do to our eating.

What should I do when I'm way, way down?

Would he ever give me too much to bear?

You mean this problem could make me stronger?

Glory in infirmity? Really?

What should I do when I'm way, way down?

". . . my heart is sick within me."
Jeremiah 8:18, RSV

"The harvest is past, the summer is ended,
and we are not saved. . . . dismay has taken
hold on me. Is there no balm in Gilead?"
vv. 20–22, RSV

"Who is . . . so wise [to] understand this?"
9:12, RSV

EVERY AMPLE SON OF ADAM, every chunky daughter of Eve, knows the feeling. Where is it getting me? Where is it getting me? I have tried so hard, Lord, and you saw what I weighed this morning. You know what I ate yesterday—the right amounts, no cheating, none. So? So I gained one pound, and what shall I say?

"Dismay has taken hold on me. . . . Is there no balm in Gilead?"

Charming lament, straight from the Word of the Lord,

103

and most of us know it by way of a lovely anthem, "There Is a Balm in Gilead." Sing it slow, sing it often. Some days I especially need assurance, and this is one of those days. I behaved myself yesterday and didn't lose.

Chapters 8 and 9 of Jeremiah comprise a classic elegy to despair. No matter what the human problem, these words touch sensitive strings. Especially if we're among the waistline watchers, they come right off the page to meet us. 'Oh that . . . my eyes [were] a fountain of tears' " (Jer. 9:1, RSV).

Jeremiah has been taking inventory. He has worked diligently, dreamed big dreams. Now summer is ended, the harvest has come and gone, and there is so little to show for his effort.

The "balm" of Jeremiah 9:22 was a medicine base from the Styrax tree. It was the balm of hope, symbol of recovery.

Was Jeremiah speaking literally? Were there actually no Styrax trees that year? Or could it be that he was so far down in the blackness he couldn't see the Styrax tree? Some days we are blind to hope; these are the times for wallowing. "Dismay has taken hold on me." Some days I like dismay; some days I love it.

What can we do with these days?

Taking our cue from Jeremiah, one thing we can do is to tell God exactly how we're feeling. Most of the prophets— and Jeremiah was no exception—seemed to operate on this basis: "Whatever I feel, I tell the Lord."

As any student of Scripture knows, this is one sure mark of God's finest. Abraham, David, Job, Amos, Hosea, the disciples, even Jesus. Is there any more realistic surfacing of pain than the famous cry of the Master, "My God, my God, why?"

From now on when I feel bad, maybe I should quit feeling bad because I feel bad. When I have been giving it my best, when I seem to be getting nowhere, I must do what the great ones—and the Greatest One—did. I must take my despair to the heavenly throne and let my Lord know exactly how I'm feeling.

> *Prayer:*
> *Lord, thank you for inviting me to tell it like it is, even on my down days. "Behold, and see if there be any sorrow like unto my sorrow. . . . My heart is sick within me. . . . Dismay has taken hold on me. . . . Who is so wise to understand this?"*
> *You are, Lord, and I thank you.*
> *Amen*

For superb therapy in the heavy times, another suggestion: Proceed to a careful study of all those verses in the Psalms with any such reference as "I cried and the Lord heard."

Would he ever give me too much to bear?

> *"As thy days, so shall thy strength be."*
> Deuteronomy 33:25, KJV

HERE IN DEUTERONOMY 33 Moses is about to die. He is prophesying for each of the tribes of Israel, and these words of Deuteronomy 33:25 are for Asher. Asher's territory is far to the north. It's not such a bad country, really, but if Israel were attacked, Asher and his people would be the most vulnerable, the first in line to do battle. "Yet you can depend on it, Asher," the old man says. "As your days, so shall your strength be. You remain faithful, and by whatever time the enemy arrives, the Lord will have you ready."

I like that. I like every passage of Scripture which assures me that my Lord is stronger than the enemy. I also like to hear him say he will meet my negatives with me.

This is an especially fine assurance when I am hesitating to look where the enemy is—inside me! The saints speak often of prayer for insight, and that is one hard prayer for fatties like us.

Why do we hesitate to pray for an honest look inside ourselves? Isn't this one reason? We are afraid the truth will overpower us. What if we ask him for the facts and he gives us too much to bear?

"Never fear," comes today's good word. "You pray for insight and I will fit my revelation to your readiness. I will never overload you. As thy days so shall thy strength be."

One day in my reading I was doing the dodging act. "What if I asked for the full load of truth and the full load buried me?" Then as I was excusing, rationalizing, putting off, I remembered a quote from one of my favorite "take-me-apart" writers. Isn't it uncanny how the Lord moves in our memory, adding one thought to another until there is no escape. That's what he seemed to be doing now. Loud and clear came this word from a mystic writing almost three centuries ago:

Now God, who is infinitely wise, only gives us knowledge of ourselves gradually and by degrees; he does not show us our misery all at once—such a sight would drive us to despair, and we should not have strength to bear it—but he shows us first of all our most glaring faults, and as we go on correcting these, he releases to us our more subtle and secret faults, till

107

at last he lays bare all the innermost recesses of our hearts. And this goes on our whole life long.*

Prayer:

Lord, I do want to see my negatives. Clearly. All of them. When you have shown me the beauty in me, show me the not so beautiful. But thanks for your love in pacing.

I know that you know all there is to know for my recovery. I know that You know too how much I can stand to know right now. Thank you for this one more certain sign of your special love for me.

Amen

---

* Jean Grou, *Manual for Interior Souls*, (London: Burns & Oats, 1955), p. 109. Although the book was compiled in 1955, Grou lived in the 1700s.

You mean this problem could make me stronger?

> *"It is good for me that I have*
> *been afflicted."*
> *Psalm 119:71,* KJV

IN AN OKLAHOMA TOWN where I was pastor, they told this story.

A wealthy oil man, with more money than he could possibly spend, decided to build a mansion for himself. This would be a showplace, too, for the citizens to "oh and ah." It was to have a stone exterior, decorated with the finest of iron-work—fences and grills; furbishes and frills; eaves, iron gates, iron doors, little iron gargoyles.

Since the man of money wanted only the best, he imported

a master iron craftsman from Italy. When the master iron man had selected his artisans, he brought them together. He explained the overall plan and some of its details. Schedules, techniques, how to measure, how to fit—all of these he showed them. Then, at the conclusion of his instruction, he added this unusual directive:

"Hear me while I tell you how we build for permanence. If the blueprint calls for a round piece of iron, take a square piece and pound it round. If it calls for a square member, take a round piece and pound it square. Always remember, gentlemen, it is only by pounding that iron gets character."

Echoes of the psalmist, "It is good for me that I have been afflicted."

Are you sure, psalmist?

Last night I saw an airline's ad for its Caribbean special: "Escape from it all to this lovely island. Take it easy. Soft sand. Gentle breezes. Smiling natives. Bargain rates." They even said I owe it to myself!

"Ease up." "Take it easy." All of us fatties love the word *ease*, and we especially love it when we are bearing down hard on our diets. "Easy does it." But does it do it? Or is the psalmist nearer the truth when he says, "It is good for me that I have been afflicted."

The word *afflicted* raises an honest question. "Who does the psalmist mean? Am I also among the afflicted?" To which every struggling fatty nods in affirmation: "Indeed I am among the afflicted. So long as there is food to eat and one scale to weigh on, I am thoroughly afflicted."

No question about that last half of Psalm 119:71—"I have

been afflicted!" But those first five words need some serious prayer: "It is good for me."

> *Lord, you mean this problem*
> *could make me stronger?*

Glory in infirmity? Really?

ONE OF THE CURRENT STARS in big-league baseball is a pitcher with a damaged index finger. In a freak accident some years back, he injured his pitching hand, and that one finger did not heal straight. Since the index finger is all important to the throwing of a fast ball, he thought, "This is the end. It's curtains for me."

Then one day as he was trying for a comeback, behold, new item! By gripping the ball to accommodate the crooked finger, he could make his pitch do strange things. Result?

Today he is one of the highest-paid players in professional sports.

Sound easy? It wasn't. For one thing he had to practice and practice and practice to master this new method. For another, nobody could believe what they saw. Was he "doctoring" the ball? Vaseline? Some foreign substance? Old-fashioned spitball? They also labeled him "sneaky," "freaky," and other things non-complimentary. But even more of a problem, he says, was reorienting his mind from negative to positive.

Nobody knows for certain the details of Paul's infirmity. Some say he had bad eyes, others believe he was a hunchback, still others think he limped. I think he had a weight problem. When I wrote my book, *The Fat Is in Your Head,* I included some thoughts on this possibility. I explained why I believed Paul might have been obese or at least inclined in that direction. Authors expect divergent reaction to the things they say and this was no exception. Some of my mail was even semi-hysterical. Who was I to label Paul a chubby, and how could I even infer he might have been a fatty?

I could because I believe Paul was vague for a reason. I think he was not explicit because he wanted us to be explicit. And when any fatty is explicit with 2 Corinthians 12:9, this feeling comes through. Paul could have been a fellow struggler struggling with our struggle (see *The Fat Is in Your Head,* pp. 102–104).

Yet putting aside these musings now, Paul does seem to have wrestled his problem down till he could say that he had won the victory. He had learned to glory in his infirmity that the power of Christ might come upon him.

How long has it been since I backed off from the negatives

of too many pounds to honestly ask, "What's good in this for me?"

What *is* good in it? What's the good for me, for others, for the Lord?

Today I will pray a positive prayer. I will thank God for the good things here.

> *Lord, I glory in a problem I can see.*
> *Some people have chronic hidden*
> *difficulties—*
> > *unknown, no handles.*

> *Lord, I glory in the thrill of accomplishment.*
> *Every time I lose weight, this is exciting.*
> *Lord, I glory in the help around me.*

> *Books, doctors, nutritional experts;*
> > *helpful groups, helpful movements,*
> > *helpful individuals,*
> *and especially my favorite cook—*
> > *they help me and I am grateful.*

> *Lord, I glory in the fact that mine is a*
> *problem which can be solved.*
> > *One of my friends has an incurable*
> > *disease,*
> > > *but mine can be corrected if I*
> > > *cooperate.*

*Lord, I glory in all I have learned about
    life and myself and you as I have struggled
    with my problem.*

*This is good, Lord.
    Help me "find true joy and pride
    in the very thing that is my weakness."*
                                        Amen

THE CROSS

"If anyone wants to be my disciple, he must say 'No' to self, put his cross on his shoulders, and keep on following me" (Matt. 16:24, Williams).

If! Hard word for soft people

The big *I* with minus mark

The tyranny of no vacations

Co-crucifixion

Co-resurrection

If! Hard word for soft people

"If anyone wants to be my disciple,
he must say 'No' to self, put his cross on his
shoulders, and keep on following me."
Matthew 16:24, Williams

THE FIRST MOVE in any divine-human encounter is God's move.

Jesus came to bring the Good News, every kind of Good News. But the best of his Good News is his news of the heavenly Father's never-ending search. Every day, every night; early morning, noon, late evening; always, 100 percent of the time, he moves toward all his children.

That, said Jesus, is move one.

But then comes the time, he also said, when it's our move. Move two. And the problem with move two is that so often moving toward the Father's love means moving away from other loves. People. Things. Food. Sometimes if we are to follow him it's *either-or*, not *both-and*.

Unfortunately, most of us in the girthy fellowship have long been *both-and* people. We want our cake to anticipate, to nibble, to devour; to rave about. But may it never make us fat. We want both cake *and* a slim body.

Now into this kind of lumpy thinking comes Jesus with his hard word for soft people: *"If anyone wants to be my disciple, he must say 'No.'"*

Careful now. This is a fooler. The big word here is not "no." The mighty word is that little word "if."

A very loaded word, this "if." So many trains of thought track here. "If I do this, Lord, you mean I can never ever say 'yes' to some of my old friends? Dear old friends like cookies, buttered popcorn, cashew nuts? Is that what you mean—'no' to them, 'yes' to you? If that's what you mean, can't I decide tomorrow, next month, right after my birthday?"

It's a hard word for soft people—*no*. I must take up his cross, no argument! Can't I even ask, "What's in it for me?" My Bible tells me that Abraham asked it, and Jacob, Moses, Gideon, Job. So did many other "iffers." The disciples laid it right out there: "We have left all. What do we get?"

So what *do* we get?

Here's an exercise for some more heavy thinking:

If I really did put his cross on my shoulder to keep on following him, if I began today eating what he wants me to eat, and if I kept on eating his way, these are the things I think I would get: _____

_____

_____

_____ .

Promise straight from the Lord:

"Seek ye first the kingdom of God, and his righteousness; and all these things shall be added unto you" (Matt. 6:33, KJV).

"We are at liberty to stop at any time. . . . but think what we shall feel like when we see Him if all the 'thank you' we gave Him for His unspeakable salvation was an obstinate determination to serve Him in our own way, not His."

Oswald Chambers

The big *I* with minus mark

> *"If anyone wants to be my disciple,*
> *he must say 'No' to self."*
> Matthew 16:24, Williams

> *". . . let him deny himself."*
> v. 24, KJV

> *". . . renounce self."*
> v. 24, TCNT

> *". . . disregard self."*
> v. 24, Goodspeed

> *". . . give up all right to himself."*
> v. 24, Phillips

THE CROSS: "A big *I* with minus mark."

A minister friend tells this story. He and his daughter (very wise and very small) were standing one day before the altar when she said, "Daddy, it looks like somebody took a big *I* and ran the minus mark through it."

"Out of the mouths of babes" do come sharp observations. But I have also read something akin in certain of the mystics. Once the thought was attributed to a holy nun, next time to a simple monk. Their observation: "Stand straight! Put a

123

sword through your soul, a cruel sword, and long. What have we here? The Cross."

Does it matter who said it first? I think not. Say it again; the real message is, "As a follower of the cross, I cannot always do things both my way and his!"

Always with the Christian fatty a number-one requirement for right eating is that awful word *sacrifice*.

As Bible students, should we be surprised that "sacrifice" is one of the dominant themes of our Christian faith? From early times the believer's big emphasis was "bring unto the Lord a sacrifice. Bring sheep, cattle, goats, pigeons, people. Create for Yahweh the sweet-smelling sacrifice."

So what could be the matter with this?

The matter with this, says Jesus, could be everything. If our sacrifice is mere external trappings, we have missed the central call of God. Certainly he wants the external trappings. Bank accounts, stocks, bonds, gold, houses, barns, animals; we call them ours, but they belong to him. They were his first. We are to let him know we know they are his. Then as they come into our hands, we are to offer them all for his use his way.

But for those of us in the lifelong struggle with obesity, *sacrifice* has another meaning. "If anyone wants to be my disciple, he must say 'No' at mealtime, snack time, all the time." Other translators call it "deny," "renounce," "give up," but for us by any term the meaning comes clear. Our sacrifice is associated with food. This is our cross—to eat his way.

Always for us it is exactly like the little girl said—or the nun, or the monk, or anyone telling it like it is. Our major symbol is not a table laden down with all kinds of good things. Neither is it any of the traditional symbols of history—burning bush, descending dove, protective shield, open Bible. The number-one symbol for any earnest heavy Christian is forever the Cross—

Big *I* with minus mark!

"The love of God is hard as Hell!"
Jean Pierre De Caussade

The tyranny of no vacations

"If any man will come after me, let him deny himself, and take up his cross daily . . . ."
Luke 9:23, KJV

". . . day after day . . ."
v. 23, NEB

". . . every day . . ."
v. 23, Phillips

". . . every waking moment . . ."
v. 23, C&M

Whenever all the synoptic Gospels record certain sayings of Jesus, we can make it our policy to give these triple attention.
Luke 9:23 is repeated in Mark 8:34 and Matthew 16:24. The value of this triple study comes clear when we notice that Luke adds one word missing in Matthew and Mark. This is the single word daily—and isn't that an addition just for us?

THERE IS AN EXCELLENT BEACH where we live. It goes on for three-and-a-half miles of beautiful white sand. Semi-white, actually, but still beautiful. It is also a great place to splash about on quiet days. Or if the sea is not turbulent we carry our floats and ride the waves. But we never take chances, because sometimes the beach is dangerous—and that danger comes from the undertow.

127

Undertow is a sinister threat because, almost without knowing, a swimmer can be pulled far out by it. This is exactly how it can be with the Christian's commitment. Almost without our knowing, we can be carried away in the undertow.

Most of us on the corpulent side do not find ourselves in the "perfect-little-Christian-all-at-once" crowd. Almost always we are among those who come out of great tribulation trying to make our commitment stick. And the undertow is so daily.

Luke was a physician and, being that, he set down certain prescriptions for specific needs: "Take daily. Three times daily. Before every meal."

Did you know, Luke, how tyrannical this prescription can be for the fatty?

"If any man wants to be my disciple, he must say 'No' to self, put the cross on his shoulder *daily*, and continue to follow me" (v. 23).

No vacations!

Co-crucifixion

"I am crucified with Christ."
Galatians 2:20, KJV

WE PREACH the full gospel!"

That's what the sign read, so we attended. It was a nice church, beautiful architecture, and especially beautiful windows. Furniture: oak. Pew cushions: mauve. Choir robes: mauve too. Cathedral organ, superb music. Preacher: round—very round. Stern type—very stern, but very effective. I tried, honestly I tried, to apply my finest Christian attitude. But even trying my hardest I could not keep back this one sardonic item from my memory:

The parson shakes his flabby jowls
As 'gainst the people's vice he howls.
I hear him damn their fleshly sins
Yet there they are—his three fat chins.

And who am I to point the finger? Back up, Charlie! How many sermons have you preached behind a robe to hide your weak commitment?

Hard fact! I too have been among the pretenders, preaching full surrender for each and every one in hearing range, partial surrender for me.

Some wag has said, "If all the critics of the church were laid end to end, it would be a good thing."

Maybe. Maybe not. The church is the Lord's for sure. These are his people. But so long as the church is also me, doesn't the church need someone saying with the saint, "Thou ailest here and here."

One place the church ailest for sure is in its halfway preaching of the cross. "Behold what our Lord has done for us!" Great emphasis. All important. But then comes the lost half of the theology of the cross. This is the tough theology, and I don't like it. I prefer to circle Calvary, looking up, admiring Jesus: "See what he did for all mankind, for me."

For that I am grateful, for that I praise his holy name. Then I praise some more and maybe even praise till the sound of my praise deadens another sound—the sound of his call to identify with him as he identifies with me. Identify *in toto*, with no reservations. None.

"I am crucified with Christ."

So easy to say. So hard to do. So ongoing.

Today we mean business. We take up our cross with every

good intention. Then somewhere along the way we lay it down, rest a minute, take a breather. But when we move on, we tend to leave behind our good intentions.

No wonder the Christian life has been defined as "a series of new beginnings." And no wonder, either, that for all us heavies "co-crucifixion" is never an act but an ongoing process.

> Prayer:
> Lord, today I would take the cross off Calvary's hill and erect it here at the center of my being, at the center of my appetite. Daily, every time I sit to eat, many times each day, may I understand . . . the Christian life means co-crucifixion over and over.
>
> Amen

Co-resurrection

> *"If we have been planted together*
> *in the likeness of his death, we shall be also*
> *in the likeness of his resurrection."*
> Romans 6:5, KJV

T HE WEAKEST SAINT among us . . . . can experience the power of the deity of the Son of God if once we are willing to 'let go.' Then when we have made the decision, we have to keep on letting go, and slowly and surely the great full life of God will invade us in every part."*

On first reading, that statement seems almost impudent.

---

* Oswald Chambers, *My Utmost For His Highest: The Golden Book of Oswald Chambers* (New York: Dodd, Mead & Co.), p. 103.

The life divine, mine? Mere mortal shares resurrection glory? Can it possibly be?

"Yes," says Romans 6:5, "it can be!" But here comes that big *if* again. Resurrection in its purest form means "return to life," "resurgence," "revitalization," plus so many other good things. To most of us from religious backgrounds the word *resurrection* brings with it sounds of joy, gladness, the happy heart.

These you can have, Paul tells the Romans, but *you can't have them for nothing.* The purest feeling of divine exaltation (those little everyday thrills of the spirit and the great quiet gladness of knowing him)—he only shares these with those who have shared his cross.

If we could stop any person in the street or get their attention anywhere, if we could go deep into the back rooms where they keep their dreams, if we had the time and they had the time to share their secret hopes, we would find they are true brothers and sisters at this one point:

All of us want to be happy,
to feel good,
to enjoy.

There would be other hopes—success, money, things, thrills, fame, power. But running along beside all these in the mind of any clear thinker, any deep thinker, is the haunting question, "What if I get everything I want, all of it, and it doesn't make me happy?"

One of the most startling statements I've ever heard on this theme came from a college rap session. Today's young people will go on almost forever on the "What-do-you-want-out-of-life" themes? On this particular evening we were looking to the future, discussing aims, and sharing goals. Finally the talk turned round as it always does to variations of "I want happiness" . . . "I want to feel good" . . . "I want to enjoy life." Only this time one young dreamer sounded a different note.

He was a sharp looker, obviously the leader kind, and he wanted happiness too. But he seemed to be looking past that want now, and this was his statement:

> You've got to watch this stuff. Happiness can fool you, bad. Like you should see our house. We've even got a pool inside, I mean a pool in the living room and carpet all around. But you know something? My dad knocked himself out to get all this, and is he happy? No. As a matter of fact, he's the most miserable man I know. And my mom? She's miserable too. I think she even hates the whole thing. So you know what I've decided? I've decided happiness isn't a big house and a pool inside and carpet all around. Happiness must be more like something underneath all this, something you have inside. I want that, and that's the only kind I want.

So do I. So do you. So does everyone want that particular kind.

Yet there is a fooler here too. Inside happiness cannot be had by mere wanting. Unless we understand this, we may even get what we thought we wanted and end up still wanting.

For the Christian all wanting must finally narrow down to this: We are to want what the Lord wants. Only when we have purified our wants by his wants can we know pure happiness.

There is a pensive verse in Hebrews 12:2 which illustrates this process to absolute perfection. The writer is calling us to rid our lives of anything which may be interfering with our spiritual arrival. The best way to do this, he says, is to "keep your eyes on Jesus" (TLB).

Then we are led to some deep thoughts on another deep statement: "[He] for the joy that was set before him endured the cross."

Other translators say he endured the cross:

"to win his prize of blessedness" (Knox),

"in order to reach his own appointed joy" (Moffatt),

"understanding he would feel right afterward" (C&M).

Today I *don't* want to eat his way. I want to eat what I want to eat. I do not like this cross in the center of my appetite. So eat your own way, Charlie. Do what you want to do. But this is the law of the Lord. That good feeling you want does not come by any other way than the cross.

Forever and forever by holy decree he has ordained it:

Crucifixion first,
then resurrection.

"There is not, and never can be upon this earth, any real happiness but by way of the cross."

Jean Grou

JUDGMENT

I do not like the "accounting" themes, and most of my fat friends don't either.

What is it about our problem which makes us believe we'll be exempt from the Lord's tribunal—or, at least, that we'll be exempt for a long time?

That's how we are, all of us—great girth, medium girth, even a little girthy—we prefer to go on thinking and hoping we will be excused.

Is God disappointed in me?

How will I look on the Judgment Day?

What do I think of me?

What do others see when they look at me?

Examination on my own tendency to judge

Is God disappointed in me?

> *"The eyes of the Lord are in every place,*
> *beholding the evil and the good."*
> Proverbs 15:3, KJV*

IN A CERTAIN ENGLISH CLUB, a man by the name of Crowe made himself obnoxious by constant boast of his agnosticism. Not only would he scorn those who believed, but he was forever trying to push his disbelief on the believers. Finally, when one of his fellow members could take no more, he wrote this poem and tacked it to the club bulletin board:

---

* Readers of my previous books know that Proverbs 15:3 has special meaning for me. See for instance *The Fat Is in Your Head*, p. 95.

We've heard in language highly spiced
That Crowe does not believe in Christ.
But what we're more concerned to know
Is whether Christ believes in Crowe.

Theologically speaking, of course, Christ does believe in Crowe—in the real Crowe's divine possibilities. He also believes in me, the original me. But is he disappointed? My size, my shape, my condition right now—how does he feel about the me I have let myself become?

Divine judgment is a very real part of every worthwhile religion. So is the omnipresence of God. No spot escapes his beholding and that is hard truth for our kind. Most of us have built into our thinking certain hiding places where we prefer to believe nobody knows what's going on (or what's going *in*).

I hesitate to say this, because it sounds so infantile, yet there was a time when I would say to myself, "If Martha doesn't see me, this won't make me fat." To which the weighty chorus will respond, "You didn't invent that. I did!"

Now from the wisdom of Solomon, this shocker: "The eyes of the Lord are in every place."

Question: Is this good news or bad news? Isn't it bad, bad news if we know he is watching us eat that left-over black-bottom pie? Yet isn't it good, good news if we understand God cares so much about us that he is always here, always with us. And when we search the Scripture for more on his all-seeing love, we get another feeling. The Divine eye is not a fixed eye staring us down. Second Chronicles 16:9 puts a sweep to the Father's look: "The eyes of the Lord run to and fro throughout the whole earth" (kjv).

More questions:

What difference will it make today if I remember, no matter where I am, he is watching?

No matter how far I've gone, there he'll be watching too. How will I like that?

One of our writer friends, a raiser of birds, tells this story:

One day she brought home a new cat, a fine blue-blooded cat. When she got him home, she showed him his environs. Then she took him up in her lap. Conversation: "Cat, you and I will surely be friends, but the time is now for an understanding. Due to the nature of my existence, I will sometimes be traveling, earning money for mundane things like cat food. You see then, don't you, how absolutely essential it is that you be the kind of cat who can be left alone with the canary."

Isn't that the kind of creature all of us portly children of the Lord (plus all the non-portly) must aim to be?

> "The eyes of the Lord are in every place, beholding the evil and the good."

> "The eyes of the Lord run to and fro throughout the earth."

Suggestions for added study:

Numerous times the Bible refers to "the eyes of the Lord" or "the sight of the Lord." Certain of these verses have been particularly apropos for group discussion, or for individual reflection. Here are some possibilities:

2 Samuel 15:25	"If I shall find favor in the eyes of the Lord" (KJV)—that big *IF* from another angle.
1 Kings 22:43	"doing . . . right in the eyes of the Lord" (KJV)—am I?
Psalms 34:15	"The eyes of the Lord are upon the righteous" (KJV)—and the unrighteous, too?
Amos 9:8	"Behold, the eyes of the Lord God are upon the sinful kingdom" (KJV)—answer to question raised above.
Zechariah 4:10	"The eyes of the Lord . . . run to and fro through the whole earth" (KJV)—that roving eye again.
1 Peter 3:12	Exact duplicate of Psalm 34:15—must have been meant for a double take.

How will I look on the Judgment Day?

> *"For we must all appear before the judgment seat of Christ, so that each one may receive good or evil, according to what he has done in the body."*
> *2 Corinthians 5:10,* RSV

AWESOME THOUGHT: One question at the final judgment will be, "What have I done with my body?"

Most of us in Christendom believe in a final accounting. From the church, from our parents, from our reading, the message came clear. What we heard probably varied from happy slants with golden streets and angel wings to the harder notes like "You better be good or else."

Now comes 2 Corinthians 5:10 with what may be a new question for some of us:

"Have you ever considered, fat friend, that the body you take to the judgment seat—its size, shape, condition—will be one certain criteria?"

For we must all appear before the judgment seat of Christ, so that each one may receive good or evil, *according to what he has done in the body.*

Question: Is this so bad?
Answer: Doesn't that depend on me?

To stand before the throne of God and hear him say,

"Well done, good and faithful servant.
I like the way you've cared for the body
   I gave you.
You've spent a lifetime shaping up my way,
   and I congratulate you.
Enter thou into the joy of thy Lord."

Wouldn't that be one great day?

Prayer:
Lord of all humankind—all sizes, all shapes—help me to remember that every day is judgment day. Right now as I stand before you, tell me what you think.

And as I move on toward the final judgment, help me to be shaping up for you.

Amen

What do I think of me?

"Let every man prove his own work, and then shall he have rejoicing in himself alone . . . no need to compare himself to others."
Galatians 6:4,
(KJV *and Knox combined*)

A COLLEGIATE FOOTBALL STAR was being interviewed on television. This was no ordinary player. He weighed over two hundred pounds, yet he could run the dashes in record time. A good student, he was also smart on the field.

With another year of college, he was debating. Should he, or shouldn't he accept an offer from one of the pro teams now?

When the interviewer kept pushing him about his money potential, the young man made this unusual statement: "If I go pro it won't be only for the money. It could be just because I need a new challenge and I want to get on with my life. Most people won't believe it, but money is not number one with me. Money brings you friends for a while, sure; does it bring you happiness? My mother taught me real happiness is what you think of yourself."

I was part of a conversation recently in which the talk turned to that profound statement, "Real happiness is what you think of yourself." This was a group of younger Christians, and I am always amazed how the young react to profound statements. This one they took way down for some deep, deep discussion, out of which came the conclusion, "If you really are living with the Lord, if you really are on his wavelength, then what you think of yourself and what he thinks of you could be almost the same thing."

Some may question a theology which says that self-evaluation and God-evaluation could be almost the same thing.

Yet isn't this worth thinking through?

> If I really am sensitive to the heavenly
>   Father's daily judgment,
> If I believe he created me with the capacity
>   to know right from wrong,
> If I am trying to live his way,
> Couldn't my honest opinion of me
> Be at least one reflection of his opinion of me?

For the Christ-centered, isn't this the real judgment seat? How do I look to myself today?

> *"Let every man prove his own work, and then shall he have rejoicing in himself alone . . . no need to compare himself to others."*

What do others see when they look at me?

*"Always bearing about in the body
the dying of the Lord Jesus,
that the life also of Jesus might be
manifested in our body."*
2 Corinthians 4:10, JWNT

ONE OF MY FAVORITE TEACHER FRIENDS, a seminary professor, sometimes started his classes with, "Are you a 'mind Christian' or a 'heart Christian'?"

It does make a difference, and now comes 2 Corinthians 4:10 to ask, "Are you a body Christian too?"—"Always bearing about in the body the dying of the Lord Jesus, that the life also of Jesus might be made manifest in our body."

Implication: Our first assignment is not "saying" but "being." Or to put it another way, belief in the Lord Jesus is only our starting place! The real question is, "Have I experienced him deep inside, and does my body reflect his presence there?"

Everyone has had certain moments where the waters divided and we passed over to a new place. One such for me came in a letter from Emporia, Kansas, following a speaking engagement.

I had been invited to address the monthly dinner meeting in a large Methodist church. I do not remember my subject, but I will never forget what followed. Several days later a letter arrived from one very unusual medical doctor. He said he had been invited as a guest to the Methodist dinner. He liked the theme I had announced, and he had read some of my books, so he came. But he wrote,

> I cannot tell you how disappointed I was when I first laid eyes on you. Why don't you lose one hundred pounds and then come back to give your talk? For me, what you said was completely wiped out by your appearance. You would sound so much more authentic if you looked more authentic.

Isn't it almost unbelievable how a few words rightly fit together can completely change one life? Thank you, doctor. That single paragraph will always be one turn-it-around-and-head-in-a-different-direction statement for me. Though you have long gone to heaven, one day I'll look you up to tell you all your letter meant. The devastator, the needed devastator, the start of a real conversion.

That phrase from today's verse, "the dying of the Lord Jesus" can only mean one thing here. I am to yield my will to his will. I am to yield and yield and yield until the life of Jesus is manifest in my body.

Most of us have been brought up on the importance of witness. But witness of word has its limitation. Why? Because in a real sense I can never give another person my spiritual experience. Yet I can, it says here, live with my Lord in such a way that people, seeing me, will see him.

One translator makes it even more explicit: *"Every day we experience something of the death of Jesus, so that we may also know the power of the life of Jesus in these bodies of ours"* (Phillips, emphasis mine).

The witness of our bodies is never one-time-only. This is *daily* witness—every single day, no exception.

What *do* others see when they look at me? Corpulent mass? Misshapen hulk? Over-padded Christian? Or do they see one who is living daily with the Lord, manifesting in the body divine good health?

Examination on my own tendency to judge

John 8:7

Romans 2:1

Matthew 7:1–5

Romans 4:3

John 21:22

Isaiah 51:1

Every student of the bible knows that God in his Word has a way of taking us straight down the hall to our mirror. Numerous verses in both Old Testament and New lead us to self-evaluation. In today's devotion we change pace from thinking on one particular verse to a multiple-verse examination.

1. *"He that is without sin . . . let him first cast a stone"* (John 8:7, KJV).

The last time I said something judgmental about some-one was _____.

But I think I really did have a right to say it.   Yes _____
No _____ "Well, maybe" _____

2. *"Wherein thou judgest another, thou condemnest thyself; for thou that judgest doest the same things."* (Rom. 2:1, KJV).

Those negatives I am most prone to judge in others are _____, _____, _____.
Are the psychologists right? What we judge in others, they say, is a reflection of our own faults. Is there any way it might be true that what I criticize in others could be a fault in me?   Yes _____   No _____

3. *"With what judgment ye judge, ye shall be judged"* (Matt. 7:2, KJV).

If today I should be called to my own final judgment, I would be perfectly satisfied to be judged on the basis of Matthew 7:2.   Yes _____   No _____

4. *"Why do you observe the splinter in your brother's eye and never notice the plank in your own?"* (Matt. 7:3, JB).

One tricky maneuver in minds like ours—fat minds—is the tendency to judge others for lack of control. Any problem here for me?   Yes _____   No _____
When I see someone whose appetite is obviously out of control, do I:

       Put that person down?   Yes _____
       No _____

Look with scorn? Yes _____ No _____
Do I feel genuine sympathy and pray for my fellow
struggler? Yes _____ No _____

5. ". . . *Let not him which eateth not judge him that eateth*"
   (Rom. 14:3, kjv).

   (For us fatties that means, "When you're on a diet,
   quit fussing that others can eat what you can't.")

   Do I on occasion look too much or wonder too much
   at the amount and the foods others are eating?
   Yes _____ No _____

6. "*Look to the rock from which you were hewn, and to
   the quarry from which you were digged*" (Isa. 51:1, rsv).

   Many of us with weighty problems came from backgrounds of false piety. Growing up in judgmental families,
   early on we learned the ugly art of carving up people with
   the evening roast. Or if not that, did we ever stew teachers,
   fry neighbors, bake relatives?

   On a scale of zero to ten, in this area I rate my family
   history _____.

   > The last time I asked the Lord to make me
   > less judgmental was _____.

SPECIFIC GUIDANCE FOR SPECIFIC PROBLEMS

A helpful technique for surfacing biblical helps on weighty matters can be reading the daily passage and letting it ask questions—questions about our behavior, our thinking, our eating.

It's amazing how specific the Lord will be when we ask him for specific guidance to our specific problem.

Am I letting my eyes take over?

Am I thinking too much about food?

Am I eating too much when I'm tired?

Am I alert enough to the little dangers?

Am I allowing food to destroy my relationships?

Am I overly afraid of the new?

Am I missing his presence on the big days?

Am I letting my eyes take over?

> *"If . . . thine eye be single, thy whole*
> *body shall be full of light."*
> *Matthew 6:22,* KJV

THERE IS ONE MAGNIFICENT BUFFET at The Pirate's House, a restaurant near Savannah, Georgia. Fifty feet of food selection. Super entrees—beef, pork, fish, fowl, lamb. One dozen vegetables too, plus thirty-five items in the salad selection. Then there are fruits, and some of them are laden with calories—especially those soaked with delicious, heavy dressings. Finally, there are desserts too numerous to mention. It's a true gastronomical fantasia.

Every fatty has been to some place like The Pirate's House. And every one of us knows how it goes. See this, see that, lo here, lo there, oh my, oh my, starting with the eye! All of us weighty sons and daughters do have a super eye (two super eyes) for food.

Now here comes Jesus, right out of today's verse, telling us, "If . . . thine eye be single, thy whole body shall be full of light."

What does he mean by that little word *single?* And "full of light"—what does that mean?

Two times the Bible mentions singleness of eye (Matt. 6:22, Luke 11:34), and "singleness of heart" three times (Acts 2:46, Eph. 6:5, Col. 3:22). As always, some of the new translations expand our minds with their renditions of *single:* "clear," "unclouded," "true," "sound," "healthy," "unaffected," "undivided."

But going back to the original, another meaning seems to surface. This is a meaning right on target for all of us who are pudgy and protruding. Singleness of eye and singleness of heart in purest form seem also to carry the meaning, "to sort and discard . . . to select . . . to reject . . . to choose what the eye and the heart will finally focus on."

If ever one verse weighed a ton for heavies, this is the verse, "If . . . thine eye be single, thy whole body shall be full of light."

I have one friend who lights up my life. In the light of her glow I see things I would never have seen without her. Is it mere coincidence that more than anyone I know she has focused her life on the Lord?

156

Prayer:

Lord, thank you for people who glow from right relationship with you. With all these choices before me, focus my eye where it should be focused. So may I too be lighted with your light.

Amen

Added thought about eyes and how food looks:
    Always it looks better on the table,
        behind the counter,
        in the case,
        in that ad . . .
            than it would look on me.

Am I thinking too much about food?

ONE OF MY YOUNG FRIENDS quit drinking last summer. He is an executive climbing the corporate ladder—going up fast. Perhaps the reason I am especially proud of him is that he comes from such a negative background. The happenings of his childhood and the events of his youth could have provided him every excuse to give up. Some with lesser stuff might have quit caring, quit school, quit trying.

Wally's father was an alcoholic. Isn't it interesting how that tendency does a complete reverse on some children? It certainly did on Wally. Until he reached the level where all his business associates drank, Wally wouldn't touch drop one. Then, because it was the thing to do, he began keeping the fellows company, having one now and then. It was expedient. It was acceptable. It was less of a hassle. Then he began having two, three. So what happened last summer?

Straight from Wally:

I got to the place where I began thinking about my noon martinis at ten o'clock in the morning, and that worried me. Sometimes at three in the afternoon I would catch myself over-anticipating my pre-dinner cocktail. Or shouldn't I say cocktails? You probably know what happened. The longer I put off blowing the whistle, the more I tended to welcome a drink or two, or more. Then one day a light came on and a little voice inside said, "Wally, this must be how alcoholics get their start."

But that isn't all the little voice said. It said some things about my father and how would I like my children growing up with memories like mine. It also said some things about my mother, what she went through, and what would I be doing to my wife if I let this thing get away from me.

Well, anyway you know how I believe in the Lord, and you know I believe that small voice was his voice. So now I've sworn off drinking, and it sure feels good.

Thanks, Wally, for your inspiration. Drinking is not my problem. An alcoholic I am not. But foodaholic? Yes! And do I ever identify with what you're saying. How often in the time gaps my mind turns to food.

Anticipating can be a good thing. Looking forward to dinner, to lunch, to breakfast; to the companionship of family and friends at mealtime—that is one of the Lord's great gifts. But over-anticipating is something else.

Maybe I should learn this verse and hang it in that inner chamber where the hungry me can see it often:

> "Don't keep saying,
> 'What shall we eat?' . . .
> Set your heart on his kingdom . . .
> and all these things
> will come to you
> as a matter of course."

Prayer:
Thank you, Lord, for Wally. Thank you for all the good people who listen to your voice and obey. I would be one among them.

Amen

Am I eating too much when I'm tired?

*"Jesus was tired from the long walk in the
hot sun and sat wearily beside
the well. . . . Meanwhile, the disciples
were urging [him] to eat . . .
Then Jesus explained: 'My nourishment
comes from doing the will of God.'"*
John 4:6, 31, 34, TLB

D𝗈 ʏᴏᴜ ᴛᴇɴᴅ to overeat when you're weary?

Welcome aboard!

Most of us have felt what Susan must be feeling as she
writes:

Dear Dr. Shedd:
  I have been reading your book, *The Fat Is in Your Head*,
and I wonder if you have any special advice for me in my
situation?

161

I have three children, twin boys who are five and a daughter who is almost three. (Thank heaven. Isn't two the most awful age?)

I am married to the man I love; he has a good job; we like where we live; so you might be wondering what kind of problem I could have.

Well, I will tell you. It's my weight. Right now I need to lose thirty pounds, and do you know I think I could do it if it wasn't that I get so terribly, terribly tired. All these meals to cook, this big house to keep clean, my husband to love, things going on at the church, committee meetings, car pool for kindergarten. All week millions of things seem to be whirling around my head, buzzing for attention.

So you probably know what happens. Every day it's the same thing. I start out fine, but before I know it I'm off to the kitchen for a fast food fix. Then I feel guilty, and that makes me tired again. So I eat some more.

Please, can you help me? I've always been proud of my figure and so has my husband, but you should see me now. Gross.

If I could just handle this eating too much when I'm tired, I think I could make it. Do you know what I mean? Have you ever been this way? Are there others around like me? And what did they do?

Desperately,
Susan

Do I know what you mean? Have I ever been this way? Others around like that? To which comes the same monotonous answer: "Yes. Yes. Yes!"

The Bible says Jesus was tempted like as we are, and this "energy-down, appetite-up" feeling seems to be no exception.

Today's scripture finds him in Samaria, which meant built-in heavy times for anyone like Jesus. "The Jews have no dealings with the Samaritans" (v. 9, KJV). And why? For an answer we go back to the days of Moses. On an occasion when the weary children of Israel needed help, these Samaritans had rejected Moses. They had posted their land, "No trespassing." So from that hour, for generations to come, both sides had continued a mutual rejection. With vigor.

Here now, in this land of longstanding antipathy, "Jesus therefore, being wearied with his journey, sat thus on the well" (v. 6, kjv).

Rest? Surcease from clamoring demands? No. Comes now the woman of five husbands (v. 18). Questions, questions. Talk, talk, talk. But she gets the message and runs (v. 28) to bring back a host of fellow seekers: "Then they went out of the city, and came unto him" (v. 30, kjv).

In the meantime the disciples arrived, and what did they do?

Ask any heavy! They began urging him to eat (v. 21): "Come now, have one of these." . . . "You simply must not go one minute longer without food." . . . "Here, I know you will enjoy this."

The Bible doesn't say that Jesus was hungry, but since he was tired, it does sound reasonable. "Tired *and* hungry" do travel together. *Eat* is one soothing word for the weary. And what can we do?

One sure answer is Jesus' answer. In language we can understand it comes through loud and clear. "Think heavenward. Take your mind off your appetite." Then say, "My nourishment comes from doing the will of God." (v. 34).

Sounds so impractical, doesn't it? Children screaming. Phone ringing. Husband coming home. And she should think heavenward?

Yet it *can* be done! And how do I know?

I know because countless times I've lived with "Exhibit A." When our children were small, I watched their frazzled mother drop out momentarily. In the bedroom, bathroom, attic, closet, porch, in her garden, by the gate, there she was, tuning in to her Lord. Then (sometimes less than sixty seconds later) she was back to the foray with a fresh touch, serene again, because she had been with him.

No, it never comes easy, this art of the Upward thrust. But we can develop it, work at it, until it can happen quick as a flash.

This too is among his promises: If we sincerely give ourselves to living like he lived, we can know his kind of control, including hunger control when we're weary.

Prayer:
Lord, next time I'm at my refrigerator, tired; next time I reach for the cookie jar, done in; next time I head for the cone shop, weary; help me to remember your words, "My nourishment comes from doing the will of God."
Amen

Thank you, Susan, for your phrase, "food fix." Heretofore, I've only associated that term *fix* with the drug culture. But doesn't this constant stuffing myself qualify for the same false lure? How many times have I eaten myself to a stupor? "Lord, deliver me from the 'fast food fix.' "

Am I alert enough to the little dangers?

> *"Take us the foxes, the little foxes,*
> *that spoil the vines."*
> Song of Solomon 2:15, KJV

What does this mean, this verse about the foxes, and what could it have to do with appetite?

In the Holy Land, vineyards were an important industry. A healthy economy often depended on "the fruit of the vine."

And their biggest threat? Insects? Hail? Heavy rains? No! The little foxes.

Big foxes they could trap, but the little foxes would dig under fences and go through small holes. Then they would eat the grapes and tear up the vines until they had completely ruined a vineyard.

So what is a verse like this doing in a book of devotions on weight control? How does it all fit in—foxes, little foxes, and over-eater me?

How many times have we heard it?

"This one little thing won't make you fat." One little handful of peanuts. One little sack of potato chips. One little chocolate-chip cookie. These few mints. That dab of cream in the coffee. One small bite—so small, so deadly.

Our television set went out of focus recently. The picture blurred, the sound distorted, and we missed some of our favorite programs. You know how it affects you when something goes wrong with the equipment; it's so easy to imagine the worst. And isn't it one fine feeling when it turns out to be some tiny, inexpensive item?

In this case our repairman said there was a single small break in a single connecting wire.

The next time I'm in one of those days when things are out of focus, when the image is blurred, perhaps I should check for some little break in my connections.

Little breaks, little foxes, little handfuls of this and that can ruin so much so soon and so completely.

Prayer:
"*Lord, take me the foxes, the little foxes, that spoil the vines.*"

Amen

Am I allowing food to destroy my relationships?

"Be on your guard lest your minds should ever be dulled by debauches or drunkenness or the anxieties of life."
Luke 21:34, TCNT

". . . your faculties be numbed . . ."
v. 34, Rieu

". . . with self-indulgence."
v. 34, Goodspeed

". . . with dissipation."
v. 34, Berkeley

SHE'S HURTING and for good reason. Her husband is not what he used to be. Why? She thinks it's his intake.

Dear Dr. Shedd:
    Do you think it's possible for a man's eating habits to change his entire personality? When my husband and I were first married, he was such an exciting person, so full of life, and everybody loved him. Then during the second year he began to eat too much, and sometimes he would even gorge himself. Naturally, he gained weight, and it seems as though with every pound

he grew a little duller. Today when he isn't at work he mostly sits in front of the television eating, drowsing, and finally he goes to sleep.

One night recently I couldn't even wake him. So I put a blanket over him and there he stayed till morning. I can't tell you what this does to me. It is so sad, because I can hardly believe this fun man I married could change that much. You must have known other people like this. Is there anything I can do before it's too late?

Lucy

Yes, I have known other people like this. And every time I look in the mirror, don't I see a potential candidate? A candidate for dullness down the food route.

Browsing in 2 Kings we come on a startling verse with this warning: "There is death in the pot" (4:40). True, the reference here is not to overeating, but to poison. Yet we know, don't we, that poison is of many kinds. And one of the most sinister kinds is any over-consumption which leads to the slow death of our better selves, plus the slow death of people turning us off—turning us off because we aren't any fun anymore.

The human mind is an amazing creation. Experts tell us everything we've ever learned is in there somewhere. Everything we've heard, all the happenings, all the past thoughts—they're all there. Yet marvels though our minds may be, what we do with them may be anything but marvelous.

Last night mixed in with the commercials I heard a famous athlete say, "In my sport you have to think fast. Real fast. That's why I don't do drugs. They fool you. You may think you're speeding up when you're really slowing down. Take it from me, if you want to be a winner, say 'No.'" This announcement, they said, comes by courtesy of the N.F.L.

Thank you, National Football League. I hope you reach the young people you're aiming for—plus certain seniors of us too.

I got the message. That football player's brain was made to work with lightening speed. So was mine. But how many times have I clogged the lines between me and the storehouse God gave me, the lines between me and the winner in me, the lines from me to other people. How many times have I clogged these lines with too much food?

What can you do, Lucy? It's imperative that you do something fast. I hope your husband will agree to go with you to a doctor. The medics do sometimes discover certain kinds of imbalance which can be medically corrected. If the problem is psychological, I suggest you find a good counselor or psychologist. Your man could be making himself dull to make his life more bearable.

But you can only do so much to help your husband solve his problem. Even God cannot do some things, because God has given us all—including your husband—the power of choice. One thing God will never do is to redeem our lives and other lives without cooperation.

There is no agony quite like watching some nice person self-destruct. I guess this is part of your answer, Lucy. At some spiritual crossroads we either draw closer to the Lord, or let what is destroying others destroy us too.

I hope that doesn't happen, and I would go on stubbornly praying. Even though you can't reach the husband you once knew, you can reach the Lord. Go on praying for a miracle, and I'll pray for a miracle too. I'll also send up another kind of prayer, and I hope you will too. This is the prayer for all fat folks everywhere who are cutting themselves off from their own best selves, dulled by self-indulgence.

Prayer:

Lord, there in that sad home, in that big chair, may you get through—through to the dull mind, through to restore the good man, and through to Lucy for the miracle of strength and wisdom and a better future.

And oh, God, help me to be on my guard, always.

Amen

Am I overly afraid of the new?

> *"Everyone who . . . becomes a disciple of the*
> *kingdom of Heaven is like a householder who can*
> *produce from his store both the new and the old."*
> Matthew 13:52, Phillips

LIBERAL IS AN UGLY WORD to some and *conservative* has
a negative sound for others. Yet if we truly belong to the
Lord, shouldn't we be some of each? As we muse on today's
verse two important questions rise to meet us:

Am I conservative enough to respect and cherish things
worth holding, to venerate old things worth venerating?

Am I liberal enough to look for the new, accept the new,
and respond to the Lord's fresh offerings?

And these questions suggest another: How can we know

the difference? For the Christian there is one single solid answer. Our Lord is the Lord of the eternal inventory. He alone knows what is good and what is not worth saving.

So here we are with another job for the Inner Presence. If we ask him, he will sort out and select, reject and keep. He alone can safely change the price tags. And blessed are we when we have turned over this department of life's business to him.

What does all this have to do with diets and weight control? Maybe more than we know. I, for one, have found that the longer I hang on to thoughts I should let go, the more those pounds hang on. Any stubborn refusal to yield what God wants me to yield is strictly no good. Holding on to the same old mental processes, the same old eating habits, the same old insistence on living my way may be keeping me fat. "Come weal, come woe; my status is quo" is a dangerous mindset for all of us who are over-fed and over-sized.

More than sixty times the Bible talks about "new." New fruits, new wine, new offerings, new heavens, new earth, new commandments, new creatures, new doctrines. And before the Book is done, it even goes all out to say, "Behold, I make *all* things new" (Rev. 21:5, KJV).

All things? Including this weary old diet, Lord? Yes, including this weary old diet. New touches, new combinations, new blends, new ways to prepare, to cook, to serve. Even here at my table, if I ask him, he brings from his treasure to keep me faithful.

I have also discovered this in my forty years with the same old problem. Variety in places other than at the table can be a genuine plus. New reading. New ideas. New friends.

New places. New moves. Sometimes shaking up the old familiar makes other old things we are stuck with much more bearable.

Here's an ad from a furniture salesbook:

Gone is the day when antiques must stand with antiques. Ours is a whole new era. Combined with your old furniture, new pieces bring out new beauty in the blend.

"Therefore, if you really are converted and care about my kingdom, you will be like the owner of a house who treasures old things, but also welcomes the new" (Matt. 13:52, c&m).

Prayer:
Lord God of the happy surprises, I would be like Jesus. May I never be so locked into yesterday that I miss your good today.
Give me a reverence for old things and may the blend of old and new bring out true beauty.
Amen

"How's a body going to learn if they put up fences around the timely subjects and won't let their brains graze in 'em none at all?" (from a country saint who, though she lacked in formal education, was very astute in the art of developing personal wisdom.)

Am I missing his presence on the big days?

> *"But something held their eyes from seeing who it was."*
> *Luke 24:16,* NEB

Hᴀᴠᴇ ʏᴏᴜ ᴇᴠᴇʀ ʜᴀᴅ this experience? Some major event of the Christian year came and went and you never did get in the spirit.

Dana is a stewardess for Northwest Airlines. She is beautiful and radiant—exactly what you would want a Christian stewardess to be.

Dana is also a thinker. From one of her recent letters comes this provocative observation:

I do so dread flying at the holidays. Everyone seems so anxious and weary, angry and sad. Have you ever noticed when you're flying at holiday time that you seldom see a smiling face? Even at Christmas and Easter—it's true then too. Isn't that too bad? You know some of these people must be Christians, and for them these should be the most glorious times of the year, times to really celebrate.

Knowing Dana, I'm sure she ministers to the anxious, and weary, angry, and sad. Because she is a praying person, I am sure too that she asks to be a special blessing on these special days.

Today's post-Easter Scripture sounds a note so much like Dana's. The disciples were on the road to Emmaus in great despair. Yet the Lord was right there with them. He walked with them, talked with them, stayed with them all their way. Then when they came to their own gate, "He acted as though he was going on" (v. 28, Goodspeed).

When we put our ear down to the story now, we pick up once again this old familiar note. The amazing courtesy of our Lord is one of his major features. Once he's in, he may rearrange and work us over—on a holiday or otherwise. He likes things his way, and he doesn't hesitate to say so. He may even make comments, tell us what he likes or doesn't like about our holiday eating. Our holiday eating? He wants to be Lord of our holiday eating too? Yes, that's the way it is. But whether he comes in on holiday or any day, it is always by our invitation.

I love our Easter family brunch. Ham, raisin sauce, hot cross buns, Easter candies, Easter cookies.

Thanksgiving? Oh, you turkey and dressing, sweet potatoes and pumpkin pie, cranberry concoctions and some more pie—this time mincemeat pie.

Christmas? Roast goose, wild rice, fruitcake, plum pudding, nuts, cheese, petit fours, and that ever-present box of chocolates in the corner.

All these special holidays, all these I love. But the question is, will this particular holiday be a holiday from good sense, a holiday from thinking straight about my eating, a holiday from my Lord?

Prayer:

Heavenly Father, this is a confession. So often at the big events, I am tempted to focus on edibles. Then when the major event is past, I realize I missed you.

Forgive me for going down at high times. This year help me to come away from the big days feeling, "Wasn't that a great time with my Lord?"

Amen

Thank you, Lord, for your promise:
"If you are willing and obedient,
you shall eat the good of the land."
Isaiah 1:19, RSV

"My soul will feast
        and be satisfied,
And I will sing
        glad songs of praise to you."
Psalm 63:4, TEV

Other great products by Charlie Shedd now available from Word Publishing . . .